AF267617

An Invitation to Quaker Eldering: On Being Faithful to the Ministry of Spiritual Nurture among Friends

Elaine Emily

and

Mary Kay Glazer

with

Janet Gibian Hough

and

Bruce Neumann

Inner Light Books
San Francisco, California
2022

An Invitation to Quaker Eldering:
On Being Faithful to the Ministry of Spiritual
Nurture among Friends

© 2022 Elaine Emily and Mary Kay Glazer
All rights reserved

Except for brief quotations, no part of this publication may be reproduced, stored in a retrieval system, or transmitted in any form or by any means, electronic, mechanical, photocopying, recording, or otherwise, without prior written permission.

Scripture quotations marked NRSV are from the New Revised Standard Version Bible, copyright © 1989 National Council of the Churches of Christ in the United States of America. Used by permission. All rights reserved worldwide.

The Scripture quotation marked MSG is taken from *The Message*. Copyright 1993, 2002, 2018 by Eugene H. Peterson. Used by permission of NavPress. All rights reserved. Represented by Tyndale House Publishers.

Editor: Charles Martin
Copy editor: Kathy McKay
Layout and design: Matt Kelsey

Published by Inner Light Books
San Francisco, California
www.innerlightbooks.com
editor@innerlightbooks.com

Library of Congress Control Number: 2022942605

ISBN 978-1-7370112-6-2 (hardcover)
ISBN 978-1-7370112-7-9 (paperback)
ISBN 978-1-7370112-8-6 (eBook)

Acknowledgments

We (Elaine and Mary Kay) are deeply grateful to Friend Bruce Neumann and Friend Janet Gibian Hough. Without them, this book would not have made it into your hands. The journey began when Bruce felt a leading to speak with Elaine about writing a book on eldering among Friends today. Bruce's wise input, project management skills, and gifts of eldering helped shepherd the book into being. When Janet joined the project, we suddenly had an access point to the many resources on Quaker eldering. Janet has an uncanny ability to locate these resources, which means they were available to enrich our book. We continue to be in awe of how thoroughly she tended to the citations, making sure everyone was properly credited for their contributions. She also brought her gifts of eldering to the project. Both Janet and Bruce were superstars when it came to editing the book and hashing out ideas. This was all in addition to their written contributions. Plus, the four of us met regularly for worship and work, which for over a year meant twice-weekly worship and work sessions. These few words do not even come close to reflecting how integral Bruce and Janet were to the creation of this book. Whatever you find fruitful in this book, there is no doubt that Bruce and Janet have imprinted it in some way.

We also have big, big thanks for Mica Estrada and Carl Magruder. In addition to their contributions in these pages, they gave editing suggestions that greatly improved the book. Mica, Carl, Janet, Bruce—for all you have done to help bring this book into being, and for your friendship—thank you.

So very many people have contributed their wisdom to this book. They have generously shared their experience of elders and eldering, enriching and expanding our understanding of this vital ministry. There are many stories of eldering in this book that we hope will also enrich your understanding of the ministry of eldering. You may think that some stories sound familiar. While you may think you know who they are about even when names are not used, that will probably not be the case. These stories show the commonalities of our walk in the Spirit. Plus, we have taken great care, when needed, to protect people's privacy. That has included changing identifying details at times.

Additional buckets of gratitude to Friend Charles Martin and Friend Kathy McKay, the publisher and copy editor. Their guidance and support have been vital to this project. We are also grateful to Callid Keefe-Perry for writing the foreword.

We also lift up Jan Hoffman and all that she has done to bring the ministry of eldering into the awareness of unprogrammed meetings in the United States. Her fresh perspective on eldering has seeded what continues to blossom. For her faithfulness in speaking about eldering, we thank her.

Our gratitude for all who have walked with us on this book-writing journey: *thank you*. Your support, in whatever form, has made working on and playing with this project all the more joyful. Elaine is grateful for all of her oversight/anchor committees since 1995, from Orange Grove Meeting in Pasadena, California, up to today (2022) in Strawberry Creek, in Berkeley, California. Mary Kay has a heart full of gratitude for all who have accompanied her, and especially for Elaine. After Elaine met Mary Kay at the first eldering workshop Elaine led at Powell House, in a follow-up communication Elaine invited Mary Kay to a small group of elders who gathered to tell their eldering stories. This was a pivotal moment of grace in Mary Kay's eldering journey. It also led to a long-lived, deep, wonderful friendship.

We also give thanks to Spirit, who has been ever faithful. We hope and pray that we, too, have been faithful in this endeavor. Blessings to you who have contributed to this book and to you who are reading it. Play well.

Elaine Emily and Mary Kay Glazer

Contents

Foreword

This book represents the distilled wisdom of decades of listening, accompaniment, travel, and faithfulness. I'm profoundly grateful to have been invited to write the foreword, not only because I want to celebrate such a successful distillation but also because in its pages are numerous stories that have shaped my own journey.

In the spirit of plain speech and transparency, it seems important to state that my relationship with the authors dates back to some of my earliest days among Friends. Mary Kay was a member of the first meeting I became a member of, and Bruce is a member of my current meeting. Janet and I met during a time of spiritual renewal in New York Yearly Meeting before we both moved to New England. And Elaine . . . well . . . that's a whole story in and of itself.

I read chapter 7 with fascination, seeing there the twinned story of Elaine Emily accompanying Christopher Sammond in ministry to Friends General Conference in 2002. Having discerned that they served well together, they began to travel in the ministry as a pair with some regularity. Their yoking to one another is an essential part of my own story. In April of 2005, Christopher and Elaine were invited to facilitate a retreat at my meeting. At the conclusion of that event, the two of them pulled me aside with a couple of seasoned Friends from Rochester Friends Meeting (Kenn and Lu Harper) and told me they felt I was carrying gifts of vocal ministry. If I wanted to deepen those gifts and steward them well, I was encouraged to find elders and discern how to proceed.

In Rochester Friends Meeting in 2005, most of that sentence sounded like gibberish to me. What was a Quaker elder? We have ministers? You think I'm one of them? Now what?!? It is partly what came next that makes me feel particularly excited that this book finally exists. In the years that followed, Elaine took special care to accompany members of my meeting as *they* began to accompany *me*. I eventually began to reorient my life to be better able to faithfully exercise the gifts that widening circles of Friends suggested I was carrying. Elaine did not just work with Christopher to name spiritual gifts and then leave our meeting to figure it out on our own; she was in regular correspondence with me and others in my community. We were all making it up as we went along, but we were not doing it alone. I feel some of that same spirit in this book. It is intended to help make sense of things that are not new but have not always been named well.

When I began to poke around and ask questions about the traveling ministry sometime around 2006 or so, it was not long before two books were put in my hands: Samuel Bownas's book with the very eighteenth-century title of *A Description of the Qualifications Necessary to a Gospel Minister: Advice to Ministers and Elders Among the People Called Quakers* and Brian Drayton's *On Living with a Concern for Gospel Ministry*. Bownas had written his book in the mid-1700s and Drayton had just released his a year previously. It was an exciting time. I was twenty-four years old and was hungry to learn more about the rumblings I'd heard about ministry and eldership. That there were books to read was great, even if the Bownas one was a little ye olde English-y. It never occurred to me at the time to ask if there was a contemporary companion volume on eldership that could be read next to Drayton's new work on ministry. If I *had* asked, the answer would have been "no" until the publication of the book you now hold in your hands. That it now does exist is exciting and important for the life and future of the Religious Society of Friends. It has been a long time coming, and I'm glad it has finally arrived.

As I've come to understand the situation, part of the reason a book like this hasn't been written before is because of both the complicated nature of the ministry of eldering and the painful history of authoritarianism among elders and ministers in nineteenth-century American Quakerism. As part of sharing why I'm so glad this book exists, I think it is important to talk about each of those for a bit. First up, what is it about eldering itself that may have contributed to such a long stretch without a book being written about it? Some hints can be found in the very definition this book provides:

> We define eldering as the ministry of deepening the spiritual grounding of individuals, a Quaker meeting, or other faith groups or gatherings. Elders are those who have a distinct and noticeable gift of spiritual groundedness that uplifts, deepens, and broadens the spiritual core of a meeting or gathering. When the gifts of eldering are present, Spirit often takes individuals and groups to places they might not otherwise go.

Eldering provides a kind of catalyst to ministry; it helps it to spark to life. When it does, the ministry being accompanied tends to draw the attention of those present. Often that means the nurturing ministry of eldering is less obvious than the audible offerings of someone gifted with powerful vocal ministry or a prophetic social witness. For many, the prayerful and grounding ministry of accompaniment is harder to notice than ministries of teaching, preaching, and transformative justice. This is one of the reasons I'm glad this book now exists: it draws attention to a life-giving part of our tradition that is often overlooked.

The second reason I think a book on eldering has been so long in coming is because, quite frankly, the authority of eldership was used harmfully, and I think that we have not, collectively, processed this harm. Throughout the mid- to late 1800s, there was significant internal strife within the Religious Society of Friends in the United States. Many of the splits of the Quaker "branches" emerged during this time, often as a result of gatherings of ministers and elders deciding that some idea (or some person) was not in gospel order. Exerting social pressure and spiritual rationalization led to tension and fracture. Communities and families were sometimes broken apart because of theological and social disagreements often decided upon by elders.

From my perspective, the gift of hindsight shows that a significant amount of the exercise of power in that period came from a place of fear of change and a desire to maintain the status quo, *not* from a faithful response. In the wake of those years of tension, the general trend was away from discussions of ministry and eldership, associating those terms and practices with a fraught period of Quaker history. Indeed, there are still Friends today resistant to any discussion about ministry and eldership, thinking the Religious Society would be better off abandoning those terms and the practices to which they point. Given the painful schisms and the history of misused authority, I understand that inclination. And . . . I think another way forward is possible.

I have come to think that talking about the categories of "minister" and "elder" in ways that are too rigid can become problematic. To be sure, the kinds of activities that ministry and eldering describe are indeed an important part of a thriving Religious Society of Friends. It's just that I'm not convinced that there are separate shores upon which elders and ministers stand and that their constellations of gifts are entirely different. I think there are a variety of gifts and they manifest across a continuum. I've come to this position after reflecting on the issue from biblical and historical perspectives as well as my own experience.

Biblically, there is significant overlap between the terms that in English are often translated as "elder" (*presbuteros:* πρεσβύτερος); "pastor" (*poimén:* ποιμήν); "overseer" (*episkopos:* ἐπίσκοπος); and "minister" (*leitourgos:* λειτουργός). There are some distinctions, but there are also places where the terms seem to refer to similar dynamics. For example, in Acts 20, Paul calls for the elders (*presbuteroi*) of Ephesus. Then, once Paul gets to Ephesus he meets with these folks, and while in conversation with them he informs them that the Holy Spirit has made them supervisors (*episkopoi*) and then orders them to pastor (*poimaino*) the church at Ephesus. While there are differences between the kinds of service being named, these roles are not always siloed off from one another with clear and solid distinctions. This was true among Friends as well.

In the first decades of the Religious Society, "elders" were simply ministers whose service had a long track record and exerted a formative influence on the shape and direction of Friends. It wasn't until the middle of the eighteenth century that we began to name elders who were not already recognized as ministers. These days, when talking about the particulars of a meeting community I'm far more likely to ask about who is stewarding what spiritual gifts than I am to ask who is an elder and who is a minister. This is part of the reason why I'm so pleased that this book exists. It is indeed an "invitation to Quaker eldering."

Rather than some kind of field guide to the rarefied and mythical creature known as an "elder," this book recognizes that eldering is a practice. Will some likely be more equipped for it than others and dedicate time and prayer to deepening in that work? Almost certainly. Does it make sense to call those folks elders? Sure. But that practice isn't based on some secret wisdom; it is about listening and being attentive to what more is possible, being present to the sometimes small and subtle motions of the still small voice of God. This text is not a treatise, a manifesto, or a manual. It is an invitation to consider that you—or some in your community—may be called to the steady work of walking with others, accompanying them as they explore how they are led. A book like this helps to normalize intuitive and sympathetic experiences and ways of being, letting those who read it and see themselves in these pages know that they are not alone.

I was grateful to note that the authors wrote this book knowing that they are writing in the midst of change. As they say, "[T]here is something new rising up among Friends. . . . This new emergence of eldering is bubbling up to meet the needs of our times." They know that "there is no going back to the Quakerism of yore," but they also recognize that learning about the experiences of those who have come before can be powerful and affirming for those who are to come. This book is an encouragement for a culture of eldering that isn't a nostalgic attempt to recreate an imagined past but a way for the communities of today to pay greater attention to the gifts of nurture, support, prayer, and insight.

Throughout the book there is a theme of interconnectedness and the ways in which we all may have something to learn from resting in the wilderness. Yes, the ministry of accompaniment is about support and prayer, but it is also about encouragement to follow God's leadings even when we're not sure we know what comes next. The blessing of eldering is the realization that as we find our way in the wilderness, looking for rivers in the desert, we will not need to go alone. My thanks to the authors for this invitation and to all of you reading it for the ways in which you already do and will walk with those you love and serve alongside.

Callid Keefe-Perry
Three Rivers Worship Group, Fresh Pond Monthly Meeting,
Cambridge, Massachusetts

Introduction

This book has its origins in a simple yes—in fact, in many yeses over many years. It also has roots in questions and curiosity about the Quaker practice and ministry of eldering— our own questions as well as questions from other Friends. This book will help guide, enrich, and nourish elders both seasoned in the gift and new to it. It may also open new understandings for meetings who want to encourage and support the elders among them, whether they are formally named or not. Each chapter ends with queries for reflection and discussion to aid readers in connecting with their own experience and understanding. Also to that end, we have included many varied stories from elders and others to illustrate the breadth and the depth of experience. We hope the queries and stories will lead to openings in this vital ministry for individuals and meetings.

The process of bringing this book to birth is one that has eldering at its foundation. It is a journey that began with a simple yes—a yes from each of the four of us who ultimately worked on the creation of this book. We each have served in the ministry of eldering among Friends and sometimes in non-Quaker settings.

For each of us, the journey to and through the process has been a spiritual undertaking. The preparation has taken place in us over the past twenty years or more, even though we did not know this equipping would lead to a book. Elaine Emily's call into eldering came through her work in a variety of Christian churches with Ched Myers, an activist theologian with whom she co-founded Bartimaeus Cooperative Ministries. Mary Kay Glazer, Bruce Neumann, and Janet Gibian Hough have all participated in School of the Spirit programs. We all have had life experiences, deep learnings, and God moments throughout our lives that have brought us to this moment and these words.

The process of writing this book has involved questioning and doubts and tensions; submitting to the process, to each other, and to Spirit; and feeling the energy and the joy of the work and our deepening connections to each other. Since none of us is an experienced book author, we learned as went along, sometimes bumbling, sometimes soaring.

Each of us had a different path to and through this book and a different process as we were each drawn into this project. Our roles shifted and twined from writer to elder and in other ways that felt relevant to the context of the book and to what we believe Spirit has called forth from us. In the end, Mary Kay and Elaine were the authors and Janet and Bruce served as elders, among their other roles vital to the project. We believe that how God worked in and through each of us in this work may be illuminating for others. Thus, in appendix 1 we share our individual stories for those who are interested.

Chapter 1

An Invitation

It starts with an invitation.

There is an invitation to all—to each and every one of us—an invitation into the deeper, wider, bigger places of faith. Tending to this invitation is at the heart of Quaker eldering, which has long been part of the Quaker tradition. The invitation is ever present, always calling us into an ongoing process of being formed into the communities and individuals we were created to be.

That has been true for the authors of this book, too. From the beginning, this project has felt like an invitation to adventure. Much of it has felt like a wandering exploration of "elder land"—going deep into the weeds of the many facets of eldering, some historic, a lot of it current, some in between, all with an eye to the future of our faith tradition, the Religious Society of Friends, and the world.

From the beginning, it has been our sense that there is a yearning and need among Friends for a book about the Quaker spiritual practice and discipline of eldering. We also have the sense that there is something new rising up among Friends; perhaps it is already showing itself. This new thing is, of course, part of a continuum, an evolution from the earliest mani-festations of eldering among Quakers. This new emergence of eldering is bubbling up to meet the needs of our times. While there is no going back to the Quakerism of yore, we do have within us the same Spirit that has always brought forth the gifts of eldering among Friends. We hope this book will help people recognize and develop the gift of eldering, both within themselves and within their meetings.

Eldering: Defining the Elusive

We define eldering as the ministry of deepening the spiritual grounding of individuals, a Quaker meeting, or other faith groups or gatherings. Elders are those who have a distinct and noticeable gift of spiritual groundedness that uplifts, deepens, and broadens the spiritual core of a meeting or gathering. When the gifts of eldering are present, Spirit often takes individuals and groups to places they might not otherwise go. Quaker eldering is not connected with chronological age. Some come to the gift very young, and others never develop the gift past a basic capacity.

The heart and soul of eldering is spiritual formation, nurture, encouragement, accompaniment, accountability, and, to use an early Quaker word, rebuking. Quaker meetings and groups rely on people who have great spiritual grounding or depth, who have what might be called a charism in spiritual nurture. By charism, we mean a spiritual grace or gift laid upon an individual for the sake and benefit of their faith community and even beyond. Those steeped in the gift of eldering are typically spiritually grounded, wise in discernment, tender and brave when there are divisions and conflict, and willing to offer a course correction when needed. Eldering also includes the accompanying of individuals and groups going through spiritually rocky times as well as worshipfully holding groups and individuals during fruitful times to amplify what Spirit might be calling forth. Elders also hold sacred space into which vocal ministry may arise.

Reflections on Eldering

Friends' concept of eldership focuses on the spiritual health, the interior Way to and with God, of individuals and faith communities. Elders have gifts of spiritual discernment and nurture, which are strengthened by learning, practice, and collective discernment with other seasoned members of the meeting. Their means is prayerful listening, deep listening to what is being said by another, by others, or within gatherings for worship, business, clearness, etc. where the intention is to seek the Will of God.

Chapter 1: An Invitation

Whereas the vocal minister gives birth to a message from God, the elder seeks to maintain the right conditions for birth.[1]

Katharine Jacobsen, 1931–2017

*****

We understand elders as Friends who hold a deep concern for the spiritual life of the meeting, and who carry gifts of prayer, discernment, recognizing and naming spiritual gifts, voicing hard truths, listening, teaching, a ministry of presence, spiritual accompaniment, and an understanding of the spiritual basis of Friends' faith and practice.[2]

Lu Harper
Rochester Friends Meeting, New York

*****

I have come to understand the process of eldering as discernment of the spiritual condition of each of the members of the faith community as revealed by their vocal ministry and other signs. An elder's goal is not the correction of a person's behavior but an improvement of their spiritual direction and health. What sincere seeker would not welcome such assistance?[3]

Lloyd Lee Wilson
Friendship Friends Meeting,
Greensboro, North Carolina

*****

The closest I come to explaining Spirit-led eldering is to refer to its essence, which is grace-filled. It is a sacred point of view, a way of seeing that can penetrate any experience, any structure, any situation and, by nature of its expression, help us to regain or maintain our capacity for being spiritually grounded and faithfully connected to the Spirit and to each other. But what is Spirit-led eldering? It is offering spiritual leadership, which is to support and encourage the life of the Spirit in an individual or group, or to raise questions and explore, with another person or group, ways in which they may be more faithful to the Spirit, or it is simply being prayerfully present. . . . Being Spirit-led is key. Without having this intention, we are likely to speak merely from our self-centered thoughts and feelings or from unresolved personal issues. . . .

Spirit-led eldering can be either spontaneous or intentional. It can be affirmative and supportive, or it can boldly interrupt an oppressive, negative, or violent pattern in an appropriate and workable way.[4]

Margery Mears Larrabee, 1919–2008

Since many of our Quaker meetings no longer formally or even informally name elders, you may think you don't have any elders in your meeting. Our belief, though, is that almost all meetings do in fact have elders, whether or not they are explicitly named. The elders are those who typically get asked to sit on clearness committees and on care and accountability committees. They are often the people who are asked to be on ministry and counsel committees. Elders are the people in your meeting who always come early to worship to "warm up the room." They travel with Friends called into public ministry. In addition, elders name people's gifts, and they can name the spiritual truth and condition of a gathered community. Think of who you would want to talk and pray with concerning a knotty dilemma; that person is likely a spiritual elder.

Reflections on Eldering

When I came to Brooklyn Monthly Meeting, it would not single out people as elders and ministers. But Diane Bonner was one of the people that was trying to remind the meeting of early Quaker practices and that, yes indeed, we did name people who had these gifts. And that, in fact, certain people do have gifts of many different kinds. Even the gift of flower arrangement for the flowers, you know. It was that sort of thing.

When I first came to that meeting, I introduced myself to them and told them I had been sitting with the Buddhists for a while. And someone came up to me with a pamphlet from Pendle Hill about Buddhism and Quakerism. After listening to Diane, who was definitely an elder and had the gifts of eldering in the sense of knowing Quaker faith and practice, I went up to her and asked her if she would mentor me. And she said back to me, "Well, perhaps we could mentor each other." And I said to her, "No, I need you to mentor me, and that's what I'm asking you, if you would take that on." And she did. I think she still had the sense that we would mentor each other. And I think she recognized my spiritual gifts right then and there.

I remember sometime later, a year later or something, we were at yearly meeting, and she was introducing me to somebody out of our meeting, a group of people, and she said to one person in particular, "This man is a very spiritual person." So, in that sense of naming in other people their gifts, she was an elder.[5]

Joseph Garren
Middlebury Friends Meeting, Vermont

What Eldering Is Not

Some people who reject eldering see it narrowly as finger-wagging. And, some spiritually immature people do in fact use eldering to try to keep people and meetings in accordance with an explicit or implicit Quaker order. This sometimes manifests as "drive-by eldering," where a person scolds someone for some perceived misbehavior, then scoots off and thinks their work is done—when, actually, great harm has been done. Those who see eldering as maintaining adherence to a kind of Quaker purity are usually protecting the system and the status quo rather than tending to the spiritual life of the person and the meeting. There are times when correction is needed. If so, it is crucial to take time in discernment about how to address the issue in a way that is loving and nurturing. It does not help a meeting to avoid the conflict that may come with those times of correction, just as it is not helpful to barge into it unprepared spiritually or psychologically.

In this book, we are inviting people into a more expansive and true understanding of eldering, beyond the narrow definition of criticism. We invite the reader into an ongoing conversation on this topic.

We acknowledge that different branches of Quakerism understand the role of elders and eldering in different ways. Differences in understanding also occur among different yearly meetings in the same branch and even among different monthly meetings in the same yearly meeting. Our hope is that Quakers will increasingly use the words elder, eldering, and eldership and their related actions in their best sense rather than in their worst sense.

Eldering Bubbling Up

Elaine Emily began to notice in the early 2000s that eldering was showing up in new ways among Friends. As she encountered this movement within herself and others, she felt a leading to create space for elders to tell their stories. In 2006, it came to her to gather a small group of elders together to "share our eldering stories." Wide open question. No framing or limiting or steering the response into one direction or another. She was curious about how the eldering "thing" was bubbling up in the Religious Society of Friends anew. The names of who should be invited were given to her by Spirit; they were not always her best friends, but all were elders. She invited five elders from around the country, and four said yes: Bob Schmitt, Mary Kay Glazer, Cathy Walling, and Gordon Bishop. The invitation was to come to Berkeley and gather from Thursday evening through Sunday. All paid their own transportation. Each took a turn telling their story, which was videoed and later transcribed. As they listened deeply to each other, they bookmarked anything that anyone wanted to explore more, and later they had that conversation, videoed as well.

Elaine's Oversight Committee knew she was doing this, although the project wasn't formally under the care of any group or ministry. The participants told their stories with no holds barred. They named names and gatherings. They held up the sacred, including the good, the bad, and the ugly. They told experiences of the Adversary. They named their own christening into the work. They affirmed each other. They were awestruck by the faithfulness they had witnessed and accompanied in their meetings and the ministry they had accompanied. They heard each other's confessions of where they had fallen short.

For these five elders, it was a glorious event. They felt seen and heard and so much less lonely in their faithfulness. On this strange journey, they had also built a network for themselves to test further branching out in the work.

Those videos and transcripts helped seed this book many years later. Other small groups were convened around the country, in the Northeast, Midwest, and South. These were recorded in audio, not video. Elaine suggests that the gathering in Berkeley might have been somewhat like the early Quakers' gatherings of ministers, elders, and overseers.

We think the early 2000s was the start of a re-wilding taking place in the Religious Society of Friends. One example is the advent of the Traveling Ministries program of Friends General Conference. That program brought the concept of traveling ministers and elders into the foreground for many North American Quakers. Many other programs, such as School of the Spirit and Way of the Spirit, were also seedbeds.

A spiritual hunger was arising to know more, to be more, and to do more regarding ministry. A hunger like this almost always leads to the wilder spiritual habitats.

Many Quaker ministers and prophets are arising. Currently, the people doing climate and anti-racism work are in the spiritual wilderness. Peace work, long a part of Quaker history, continues more urgently. Wherever Quakers are pushing up against the powers and principalities, that is the untamed space where Quaker ministers, prophets, and elders are to be found.

We believe elders are and will be needed in new ways in the spiritual seasons to come.

Queries for Reflection and Discussion

- What is your experience of Quaker eldering?

- Do you notice any invitations from Spirit moving within you regarding eldering?

Interlude 1

To Elder: The Verb Reclaimed

Dorothy Henderson, Grass Valley, California
Gordon Bishop, Grass Valley, California

Elders: Historically those appointed to foster the life of the Meeting and of the individuals within the Meeting.

Eldering: The act of discouraging and/or questioning an individual's inappropriate behavior and expressions of concerns while encouraging appropriate behavior and actions.

Pacific Yearly Meeting Faith and Practice, 1985[1]

Elders were originally a part of meetings. Sometimes not known as such, they were nevertheless actively caring for the ministry of the meeting. Over time, this role became a designated person, a weighty Friend, known for walking their talk, for living in a way that was aligned with the testimonies, or the Truth as the Meeting experienced it.

Again, over time, this role became troublesome. The weight of some Friends became power within the meeting, and power untethered with discernment can do harm. In some cases, elders protected the status quo instead of following new revelation.

While the definition of an elder (noun) remained positive, as is reflected in the above definition by Pacific Yearly Meeting, the term eldering (verb) no longer referred to fostering the spiritual life of the meeting but rather became a term associated with telling another that they were doing something wrong

It is this version of what it means, not to be an elder but to do the practice of eldering, that led to both the noun and the verb being removed from the subsequent edition of Pacific Yearly Meeting's *Faith and Practice.*

We, the Eldering Subcommittee of the Ministry Committee of Pacific Yearly Meeting are reclaiming the verb to elder. The act of reclaiming is calling us to look deeply at what it means to act as an elder, to engage in the practice of eldering.

We are not alone in this. Recently, many essays, articles, and other efforts have attempted to redefine and to reclaim this practice for our time. We offer this in that spirit, to join others within our yearly meetings and Quaker organizations who are trying to bring eldering into the twenty-first century.

To elder, in our experience, is not about identifying another's behavior as problematic and taking action, not even with the best of intentions. Rather, to elder is to be in relationship with another or with others and to be in relationship with God. We do not elder from our own knowing about what is in right order. Eldering comes from sinking down to the seed, from asking for guidance and waiting for the response.

To elder is to begin with listening. God is calling us to listen deeply. As Quakers, we are reminded that we hold this truth: there is that of God in all others. Eldering calls us to go beyond listening to the other. We are to listen to that of God in the other. Further, we are asked to listen to that of God in our own selves, our own hearts.

And if we are asked to speak, we ask in turn, "What words is God asking of me? How do I approach another? Where is the love for this other in me? What does that love look like?"

Echoing the call in Micah 6:8—to do justice, love mercy (kindness), and walk humbly with our God—[Pacific Yearly Meeting] Clerk Sandy Kewman has posed this question to us all: "What acts of love and justice are necessary for us to re-center our Society to a place of justice, of love, for all?" This is a question for the body. This is a question for the practice of eldering.

When speaking truth with love, we are building the beloved community. In turn the beloved community is our ground for engaging in the practice of eldering. In eldering we are called to accompany, to break bread with, to be in an intimate and yet public relationship with another or with others. Eldering is taking that calling to a specific moment, a specific relationship with the here and now.

When we hearken to the deepest Spirit within us and the deepest Spirit within the other, they are no longer the other. They are no longer the problem. They are our sister, our brother, and we speak truth to them with deepest love, with full relationship. We are called to love and we are called to truth in equal measure. This is the act that the body is called to as a whole. And this is the act that we understand to be the work of, the practice of, eldering.[2]

Chapter 2

Metaphors for Eldering: Gardens, Forests, and Fungi

I am the true vine, and my Father is the vinegrower. He removes every branch in me that bears no fruit. Every branch that bears fruit he prunes to make it bear more fruit.

—John 15:1–2 NRSV

Gardens. Forests. Dirt. Loam. Fungi. All are powerful metaphors used in many contexts because of humans' primal ties to the earth. Consider Adam in the biblical book of Genesis. Adam. This name is from the Hebrew word *adama*, which means earth. In the Genesis origin story, humans are created from earth. The English word "human" also has linguistic roots in words that mean earth.

Gardens. Forests. Dirt. Loam. Fungi.

These words, these concepts, reveal deep truths about Spirit and elders and about eldering as it is practiced among unprogrammed Friends in these times. Our meetings are like gardens, and elders are like gardeners. Our meetings are like old-growth forests, and elders are like wilderness guides. Spirit is like the mycorrhizal fungi, an essential yet typically unseen network of life running for miles underground, nurturing soil and plants and people. These are landscapes of the Spirit. Thus, these are landscapes that elders traverse.

In this chapter, we explore some of these metaphors, receiving what they teach us about the roles of spiritual elders in our communities and knowing that no words, no metaphors, will ever wholly contain the ineffable.

Sometimes You Need a Gardener

Imagine a flower bed in the height of summer. You notice the tallest flowers in full bloom, the buds, the colors, the textures. The gardener, who worked quietly in the early morning, is now nowhere to be seen. Still, the evidence of hands in the dirt is there, evidence of watering, fertilizing, and pruning. The best gardeners don't need a guidebook; their relationship with each plant in the garden and their intuition guide them as they tend to the beautiful whole.

Reflection on Eldering

Many things were opened, I humbly trust, in the light of Truth, and under gospel authority, to the different states of the people; yet it was a rather a season of digging and pruning, than of finding many plants ready for the watering. But I was instructively impressed, that I must be a faithful labourer in the discharge of duty, and content with my wages.[1]

Martha Routh, 1743–1817

Even in a well-tended garden, there is always something of nature's wildness and its resistance to being fully tamed. The gardener sometimes has hard and painful decisions to make. There is discernment as to which plants to nurture and which to displace. So, there are weeds to be eliminated or placed elsewhere. There is discernment as to which insects to encourage and which to shoo away. There is discernment as to which branches to keep and which to lop off, as in the passage above from the Gospel of John. We want to be clear that we are not sanctioning Quakers to be cruel to each other under a misguided understanding of eldering. Still, there is something indeed hard and painful at times in the work of elders that the Gospel of John points to. And yet that hard and painful stuff is part of the loving work of the gardener, just as much as the more tender nurture. These words from the Gospel of John are part of a longer discourse on love. They illuminate how pruning and weeding can be acts of love in a vineyard or, in our case, a garden.[2] In meetings and individuals, Spirit is the actual nurturer. The elder may help illuminate the ways that Spirit is present and active. As Friend Mica Estrada points out, in Indigenous ways, the garden and the gardener are not separate but connected. "There is relationship, not caretaking," she says.[3]

In our Quaker meetings, elders are sometimes gardeners—they do a lot of the work that is laid out in our books of faith and practice. They are often quietly, maybe invisibly, nurturing individuals, with an eye to their relationship to the body, as well as nurturing the whole. Sometimes elders' work is not so quiet and not so tender, as when there is a need for pruning; you could call it the painful work that underlies the beauty. Nurture does not always feel nurturing. If a gardener's tools are water, compost, and pruners, the elder's tools are a spiritual life grounded in regular communion with the Divine, love for the spark of God in even the most challenging person, the willingness and courage to shine a light on sin and wrongdoing, and the patience to watch the mystery unfold.

Both gardeners and elders can be tempted toward control, thinking they can completely shape the outcome of their efforts. Just as a gardener might want to put into place a plan that is not suitable to the ecological conditions of a particular place, an elder might want to steer a meeting to a spiritual landscape that would be unsuitable and, more importantly, not where Spirit is leading. In this, the act of cultivating a meeting to be something it is not meant to be might feel satisfactory to the elder but not very useful, and perhaps harmful, to the faith community. Still, just as a gardener can feel the energy of place when tending a plot, an elder who channels the guidance of Spirit and the energy of a meeting can be fruitful.

This garden imagery is lovely; it nourishes us, even if we aren't gardeners. Yet this does not tell the whole story. You may be tempted to linger here in the garden; you may want to dwell here, feeling like this is the whole story. You would be forgiven for this inclination. Forgiven, yes. And, invited to step out of the garden into something more.

Far from the Garden

Imagine now that you are far from the garden in a place of expansive wilderness—a place where spiritual seekers, in listening to Spirit, may find themselves. Elders need to be prepared to enter the wilderness, both on their own and as companions for others. Physical wilderness is an apt metaphor for the "dismantling times of our lives," according to Carolyn Metzler.[4]

While there is precious little of our earth unmarked by modern humanity, there are still some isolated places where the wild thrives. (Sometimes, Spirit may bring the wildness to your doorstep.) These places may seem inhospitable to many of us, and we may feel out of place. Yet, those of us who are drawn to wilderness sense that here in wilderness there is life in abundance. So it is in our relationship with God. As we get more and more connected with Spirit, we are less and less in that cultivated space and our connection with the Divine is less mediated and more direct, even raw. In the uncultivated places, our social norms drop away, as do our paradigms for how things "should" be. It can feel like we are going crazy. No matter how uncomfortable this may feel, the spiritual wilderness is a place of the yeasty inbreaking of the Divine into every cell and pore of our being. Here is where elders are often called into ministry.

It is a fearful thing to fall into the hands of the living God.

—Hebrews 10:31 NRSV

Reflections on Eldering

The Monthly Meetings, which after 1666 rapidly sprang up over England at the instance of Fox . . . were called into being to remedy a certain tendency, which Fox deplored, to division and deterioration from the first purity of conduct. . . . There can be little doubt that the institution of these meetings had at the time a bracing effect upon the Society, and gave it the strength that comes from a well-devised organisation. . . . But the natural result was not merely to coordinate the discernment of the community with the spiritual leadings of the individual, but to enlarge continuously, by the successive encroachments with which a system of organization aggrandizes itself, the area of conduct over which the community exerted absolute sway. The spiritual responsiveness, which had been the glory and the peril of the first age of Quakerism, slowly died down, and a conformity to the authority of the community tended to take its place. . . . At a time when the community was harried by persecution, and was holding its meetings week by week in defiance of the law, its leaders languishing in prison or the premature victims of their labours and sufferings, the members of necessity drew together, and were intolerant of any spirit of division in their midst. If the emphasis on conformity had only lasted during the stress that required it, and while the men of large vision and hope were in command, its effects would have been almost entirely good; but the very success of Fox's measures made the laying of this emphasis a permanent habit of the Society.

The standard of the leaders was preserved, but not their spirit, and the attention given to the purity of the Society, as an end in itself, directed into a narrow groove of tradition the energy which should have been given to wider service and fuller vision. The spiritual liberty of the individual Friend was henceforth only granted him along those lines of guidance which were approved by the not always very spiritual judgment of his fellow-members.[5]

William Charles Braithwaite (1862–1922)

Into the Wilds

The first steps toward the wilderness come as the soul connects more and more with the Divine. This can be a discombobulating place because the physical, concrete ties with who and what one has been begin to fray and lose their grip. Even though there may be rejoicing in what seems to be a tighter connection with God, the fear and discomfort of letting go of the known may play havoc and upend a life or a community. Just when the need for a spiritual guide is greatest, it seems we often find ourselves alone, perhaps only with books and stories from ancient times, other faith traditions, or faraway lands.

Often, this spiritual deepening occurs in the context of a major life change—a serious illness, divorce, birth of a child, death of a loved one, promotion, or layoff. While it is unwise to say that suffering and change always bring spiritual deepening, they may do so for those who have some practice, some framework of belief, and, if they are lucky, an elder as a companion.

Reflections on Eldering

Wilderness is a physical landscape in which we are vulnerable and in which there are no guarantees and is also a metaphor for anything in life we cannot control (illness, depression, mortality, adolescence, unemployment, war, pandemic . . .). Physical wilderness gives us a set of guidelines by which we can navigate these inner wildernesses.[6]

Carolyn Metzler

This stripping away of what cloaks and disguises our essence is painful and disorienting. The process happens over a lifetime as we learn, over and over again, to submit and surrender to the One who calls us. There might be times, at least for some people, of abrupt upheaval, a sudden thrust into the wilderness. However it happens, what is left after this divine denuding is a primitive connection with our Maker. Often, social constructs as we know them are cast aside. Michele Tarter in her 2004 essay "Go North!" vividly describes the physical, emotional, ecstatic, mystical experience of early Friends. Many Quakers, some in authority, were certainly uncomfortable with those untamed motions back then, to the point that much of it was eliminated from Quaker history, as Tarter illustrates. Friends often still seem uncomfortable with even the few tendrils of Quaker wildness that remain today and continue to sprout.

The reason for the discomfort is in no small part because this spiritual upending may look to some as unhinged. For that reason, this journey greatly benefits from elders who have the knowledge and capacity to accompany a soul into the wilds of spiritual growth. This raw, untamed connection to God is a personal and communal gift to the body of Friends—a trip from a cultivated land into less civilized parts of ourselves. Those standing vigil with and for a person having such an experience need to have some knowledge of psychological and spiritual journeys. They are also a bridge to the concrete, physical world—not to pull the sojourner back into the "real world" but to be a connection for the sojourner between the liminal forest space and the ordinary world that most of us usually inhabit. The spiritual companions can help ensure that the sojourner continues to tend to their physical well-being. Elders can also provide a place where the person can focus on what the Divine is revealing to them. Fear and avoidance on either side, but especially on the part of the elder, is likely to stop this process. Elders who have done their own internal spiritual and psychological work in the wilds can be helpful in a soul trip into the wilderness.

> By night, we hasten in darkness,
> to search for living water,
> only our thirst leads us onward,
> only our thirst leads us onward.

—"De Noche Iremos"[7]

This wilderness experience is a different phenomenon from the experience of folks who are simply disruptive or those struggling with mental illness, even though intense encounters with the Creator may look and sound like mental illness and are certainly disruptive. This is not to say that mental illness and a great spiritual event or mystical experience cannot and do not co-exist. Accompanying someone experiencing such a close encounter calls for the elder to sink deep into the fungi, so to speak, and to be willing to open more fully to the fecundity of wild space. Eldering calls for the gift of discernment and the ability to see if the fruits of the Spirit are present. If an elder is not sure whether mental illness is present and needs tending, it can be helpful to consult with other elders and mental health professionals. The presence of mental illness does not preclude faithfulness as there is that of God in every person, sometimes so much faith that it is difficult to hold.

Some people are so afraid of intense spiritual experiences and mental illness that they try to stop both others and themselves from going into the spiritual wilderness. This is even true of people who have had intense spiritual experiences themselves; they are often suspicious of other peoples' experiences, more willing to label them mental health issues rather than authentic spiritual experiences different from their own. Sometimes, spiritual transformation can look like mental illness but is not. The stripping away of what clothes and disguises our essence is painful and disorienting. What is left is a primitive connection with our Maker.

Stand still and breathe in the primal forest for a bit. Ground yourself in the undomesticated mystery of it all. You may feel as ancient as the trees, the earth, the air. Here, your innermost self may begin to break free of its fetters as it touches the untouchable soul of the planet. Stand here and learn from the Ancient One. And then, notice what pulses beneath your feet, beneath the dirt where you stand. See if you can feel the fungi, the neural network of the forest.

Reflections on Eldering

I deeply believe with everything that I am that one of the gifts of physical wilderness is how it draws us out of isolated safety and brings us to re-examine what gives our lives meaning and purpose in the larger context of the awe given us by the sheer magnitude of ocean, night sky, or wondrous fungi.

There is also wilderness in the human psyche—remote, untamed places unknown by us in any way we might recognize in this moment. Sometimes we choose to go there; we hear the invitation deep in our psyche, in our dreams, in our longing, in our boredom, and we one day turn off the phone, put the "Gone Fishin'" sign on the door, stop the mail, and head out into the unexplored landscapes of our own heart. And sometimes it is not a choice. Sometimes it is a trap door that opens without warning beneath our feet. We get a diagnosis, a shocking phone call, or an unexpected email, and our world turns inside out. The trap door opens, the abyss receives our wildly falling self, and we are in a wilderness of the soul.

Carolyn Metzler

Fungi

Underneath the wilderness forest, the fungi live. Most of us take it on faith that the unseen fungi are there, just as we take it on faith that Spirit moves among us, active in our individual lives and in the life of our community. These fungi are a big part of what makes the forest such a rich metaphor for spiritual transformation and eldering. Let us look at the amazing example of the mycorrhizae, which is a vital sort of neural network needed for the forest, and everything in it, to thrive.

According to Robin Wall Kimmerer, the author of *Braiding Sweetgrass*:

> The mycorrhizae may form fungal bridges between individual trees, so that all the trees in a forest are connected. These fungal networks appear to redistribute the wealth of carbohydrates from tree to tree. A kind of Robin Hood, they take from the rich and give to the poor so that all the trees arrive at the same carbon surplus at the same time. They weave a web of reciprocity, of giving and taking. In this way, the trees all act as one because the fungi have connected them. Through unity, survival. All flourishing is mutual. Soil, fungus, tree, squirrel, boy— all are the beneficiaries of reciprocity.[8]

Elders, with their feet deep in the mycorrhizae, can be thought of as part of the fungal bridges, part of how the people in our Quaker community stay connected, part of the "web of reciprocity," the energetic network. The spiritual gifts of Quaker elders, which we explore in the coming pages, help keep the unseen foundation of a meeting healthy so the community may thrive, as individuals and as a whole.

California Friend Carl Magruder uses his understanding of how mycorrhizae function in a forest ecosystem to shed light on how elders function in our meeting communities:

> Mycorrhizae generally are like white hairs in the soil. They bank nutrients, and move them around from tree to tree, and also serve as a 'neural net,' like a brain and nervous system. They let trees know that there is a parasite or disease in the forest and how to combat it. Like elders, the mycorrhizae nurture the things we see—instead of mushrooms, elders grow spoken ministry, faithful following of leadings, good business process—but without the mycorrhizae mat under the soil, all of these things are less vibrant, devoid of Life. Some have suggested that the great forest of the upper Midwest and Canada can be considered the world's

largest living organism because the mycorrhizae make that vast wilderness a single being. What is the spiritual equivalent? Does this stubborn fecundity undergird the Quaker movement, in all its variety?[9]

The Cultivated and the Wild in Our Meetings

Both the tended garden and the old-growth forest can be found in our meetings and in our individual lives in the Spirit. Indeed, at times we may see simultaneously the cultivated network of the garden and subterranean networks of the forest. We may wonder, especially as we move closer to the forest, What exactly are the metaphors describing? Is the elder the gardener and the meeting the garden? What then of the forest and the fungi? Are they metaphors for the Spirit? What is the elder's relationship to the forest and the fungi? When our elders and our meetings are more like gardens, those gardens may look beautiful, but they are in some way out of balance, unsustainable without tending. At times, elders, sojourners, and meetings follow Spirit into the woods, into a place that is wildly different from the garden, a place of spiritual volatility. There, we find a vibrancy in the roots, the soil, the air. We find a community of flora and fauna, and we may find in some way our spiritual home.

Carl Magruder compares the early Quakers' situation with ours:

Quakerism was born in a time of apocalypse (revelation). England went from a monarchy to a commonwealth and back again in just five years, when George Fox was 29–34 years old. England was in a mini ice age at that time, with many displaced persons moving to cities, away from old ties and ways of being. Incidentally, massive social change also characterized the time and place of the ministry of Yeshua the Nazarene, called by the conquerors "Jesus." In case you hadn't noticed, you, too, are living in a trans-apocalyptic time of the failure of institutions, disruption of the biosphere, massive wealth disparity, cultural upheaval, technological advances that outrun our ethical capacity, and a near impossibility of predicting the future with any certainty. Only a vibrant spiritual community will be able to survive these changes, and not without itself being transformed. We may also then (as we have before) make some meaningful contribution to growing humankind toward the beloved community, the peaceable kindom.[10]

For many of us, spiritual wilderness is unfamiliar. Wilderness as a metaphor may be used for any place and time that feels unfamiliar and in which we feel vulnerable, lacking a sense of control. We may be supremely uncomfortable here among the untamed—far more so than in the cultivated garden. Being vulnerable is uncomfortable, as is losing a sense of control. For some, the wild and vulnerable places are enticing. For some, they are fearful. Some get lost. Most of us, at times, avoid the vulnerability and discomfort of wild places. Thus, spiritual wilderness is foreign to us. Yet this is often part of our passage to spiritual maturity, a foundational part of our spiritual formation—going from the tame, manicured garden to the wild, untamed forest. The spiritual disciplines that Spirit uses to form us prepare us to be in the wilderness. They prepare us for a place that in some sense we cannot be fully prepared for. They prepare us for a letting go, a surrender, that Spirit may use to blow us where it will.

The cultivated garden can be appealing because of its beauty and serenity. The etymological roots of the word "cultivate" are evocative. Cultivate comes from a word meaning to revolve, to sojourn, and to dwell. We can say, then, that to live into one's gifts as an elder is to dwell in the Spirit. To dwell in the faith community. To dwell in the grace of being well used. Simultaneously, there is that sense of sojourn, a temporary stay. Even as we dwell, we are sojourners, ready to go into the wilds as Spirit moves. The etymology of the word "forest" includes a root that means doorway.[11] When our dwelling is in the Spirit rather than the garden, we may very well find ourselves walking through the gate, out of the garden, and into that which we cannot fully know and can never tame.

While writing this book, in an experience of what may be called sacred synchronicity, Friend Angela York Crane asked Elaine Emily, Joe Garren, and Mary Kay Glazer to be on a care and accountability committee for her. This came after the three of us had served on Angela's clearness committee. In the care and accountability committee's first meeting, Angela talked about how she was stumbling around in a place where she had lost all her familiar ways of connecting with Spirit. She said she was in an amorphous place in her relationship with Spirit.

In that meeting, Elaine shared her sense that the God Angela had known had to be broken in order to expand to what the God she was living into is. The image Elaine had of this process was that of a piggy bank that had to be smashed.

We had some reflection and conversation around this, with all of us expressing our sense that we didn't know where we were going or how to do this work. In other words, we were going into the wilderness, all of us unknowing and with only the barest minimum of provisions, it seemed. And yet we were also clear that this was just as it needed to be, trusting that just as a woman's body knows in itself how to give birth, so this Friend also knew how to do what Spirit was birthing in her, with the three of us accompanying her as, perhaps, spiritual doulas.

Queries for Reflection and Discussion

- What is ours as elders to tend in the garden and what is the raw life coming forth that we need to accompany and give space for?

- How do physical wilderness and fungi in particular relate to eldering among Quakers today?

- What metaphor(s) would you use for eldering?

Interlude 2

Below the Words

Valerie Nuttman

Santa Cruz Friends Meeting, California

This experience occurred when I was eldering for a minister who was part of a panel in a hybrid Zoom and in-person presentation at an academic institution.

During the gathering time there is generally a flurry of activity—introductions, Zoom checks, chitchat. Often, I'm told people are gathering early to worship. Sometimes that is true. More often, though, there are details to work out, conversations to be had.

So, I sit with the question "What is needed?" and I look for the moment when I no longer need to hear or speak and it's time to slip away and dive deep. On this particular evening, there were three presenters, and when the third arrived, she brought a little bit of chaos with her. She was in the middle of rearranging her space, clearly flustered and not ready. It felt jangly to me, like an alarm bell. I needed to go, quickly, to get underneath that noise and keep that jangly energy from touching C (the person I was elder for).

I dive, and the image I get is of the ocean. I'm diving down below the wind and the waves and the noise. Straight down into the darkness, until I reach the stillness at the bottom. There, I sit, on the soft sand. And then the tether rises up through me, out my head, and all the way up to connect to C so that he is anchored in the stillness through the center of his being. Sometimes it is more like an umbilical cord, and we are connected belly to belly, sharing nutrients, floating in space, held in a gravitational spin around a center that we can feel but not see. With this connection, we are safe and calm.

This time, though, the water is deep. A safety bubble forms around C so that he is in stillness, untouched by what is going on around him. I say a prayer that we might be in perfect alignment with Spirit and open so that the words that are spoken are clear and true, God's words not tainted by the vessel as they pass through. A golden column opens through C, and that feels like an answer. I'm so far under I feel like I'm drowning, but then I breathe in gold sparkles and they fill my lungs and spread through my body. The soft voice of Divine Love says, "Don't worry. I will be your breath." I feel held, and safe, and like it could never be any other way. Then I see the gold sparkles rising in C and I know that it's a song rising up, and at the same time my mind says, "That's silly, he won't be singing here." I know that he had some concerns going into this about not fitting well with the higher education crowd—the academics in general—and I imagine he'll want to be conservative. And still I keep watching this song building, again and again.

During this time, if time is a thing, there are two other speakers. The jangly energy continues, like static or a storm, and I am a lightning rod, taking the extra and sending it into the earth. My body twitches; my hands and sometimes my feet tingle. Sometimes I am way too hot, and sometimes I feel like ice. I stay open and allow it all to pass through. Sometimes I sway, like the water is moving me. I'm aware of words, but they don't make sense. They are not what matters now—my attention is elsewhere—and sometimes I am annoyed that they are happening.

As L speaks, agitation is evident (anxiety?) and deep wounding that is raw and asking for attention. I remind myself that my work is with C and that all I can do is keep that from sticking to him. It's very sticky and very loud.

And then S speaks and the energy drops, heavy and calm. He is the balance here.

And then it is C's turn, and the song that had been building and rising comes out clear and strong and wildly surprising. (Why is it surprising when I saw it coming?) Like a fountain? More forceful than a fountain, and also more gentle. A vibration, like a drumbeat you can feel in your body. And then the openness of the song narrows when the spoken words start, like a cough, or like it is hard to take a deep breath, and as the words wind down, down, down in a spiral, gradually the column opens out again, relaxing.

25

Note: For more reflections on eldering online, see appendices 5 and 7.

Chapter 3

Qualities of an Elder

If I speak in the tongues of mortals and of angels, but do not have love, I am a noisy gong or a clanging cymbal. And if I have prophetic powers, and understand all mysteries and all knowledge, and if I have all faith, so as to remove mountains, but do not have love, I am nothing. If I give away all my possessions, and if I hand over my body so that I may boast, but do not have love, I gain nothing.

—1 Corinthians 13:1–3 NRSV

Love was the first motion.[1]

—John Woolman, 1720–1772

Elders exhibit a wide range of skills and gifts. In our years of working with and recognizing elders, certain characteristics emerge with frequency. This chapter describes these qualities and characteristics.

Love Must Be the First Motion

So, what does it take to be a spiritual gardener? What are the qualities needed to accompany someone into the wilds? What qualities are needed for the spiritual care and accompaniment of a person, a meeting, or a ministry? Early friends named elders based on discernment regarding the characteristics that were made manifest in a person, such as spiritual maturity, gifts of discernment, and deep listening to Spirit, individuals, and groups. Some current Quaker communities still do name elders, either for a particular piece of work or for a longer season. Those who are asked to serve in this capacity usually have inherent in them some measure of the qualities that lend themselves well to the work of eldering.

As the quotes above make clear, though, love must be present in abundance because without a grounding in love, we are nothing. The hope is that this is true for all of our work in our meetings and our spiritually generated work in the world. Looking a little more closely, we see that love is made manifest in different ways depending on the kind of ministry. For elders, at their best, the motion is toward compassion, holy desire, and nurture for the meeting, which at times is an urging for Friends to live into their better selves. An elder might ask: What does this person need to recognize God's presence within? What does the meeting need to faithfully move through a particular place of struggle? How do we, with our very different perspectives, discern God's will for us as a community?

It is important to recognize that there is great peril in eldership that does not grow out of that motion of love and spiritual nurture in all its breadth and depth. Elders then and now have sometimes caused harm when they have sought to rigidly maintain tradition and the status quo rather than discerning and accompanying an individual or a meeting into that wild place of old-growth forest or wherever the Spirit may be leading. Even though most meetings today don't appoint elders, there are many Quakers who nonetheless see themselves as arbiters of what makes for a good Quaker. Sometimes acting as or perceiving themselves as elders with authority, they may do spiritual and emotional harm. They may berate, bully, and scold people or meetings, judgments that often come from their own broken places. Michele Tarter documents historical examples of heartbreaking attempts to squelch the Spirit out of early Quaker meetings.[2] The tension between maintaining traditions and adapting to changing norms and situations is still with us.

A core quality embodied by spiritual elders, then, is a deep love in the Spirit and a capacity for dwelling in the unknown, the wilderness. Add to that a deep dwelling of love in and for the community and the people in it. This love may sometimes be tender and grounding. It may also be ferocious and uprooting. While it is more comfortable to be in that tender, grounding, and nurturing place, elders also need to have the courage to stand in the tangled, untamed places when all seems lost or all is disorienting in its unfamiliarity. Elders are not standing there alone; rather, they are with the Spirit and the community, or perhaps an individual, in the midst of the wilds—possibly as a reminder of our deep roots in Christ or as a reminder that, however lost we feel, Spirit is with us.

The Eldering Fruit of Love

Other qualities grow out of that deep and fertile love. One that is especially common among Quaker elders is a keen ability to notice and name spiritual gifts present in individuals and sometimes in meetings. This is a movement of the Spirit. Perhaps you have experienced or witnessed this. If so, you no doubt know how profound this can be. There are many stories in our wider Quaker community of people feeling seen and known when an elder has named a gift in them. This can be especially true when the person is part of a community that is opposed to naming gifts or has not even considered the possibility. Many times, when an elder recognizes a spiritual gift within a person, it reveals to that person what they have already known but did not have words or a paradigm for or perhaps did not know whether it was okay to name it in themselves. When a gift is named in a person, there is often a deep sense of release that frees the use of that gift to the benefit and uplift of the community.

Reflection on Eldering

And I think it was maybe later in the day that Jan [Jan Hoffman, a traveling minister] came up to me and said, "I'm really sensing these gifts of eldering in you, and would you elder for me in addition to another friend?" . . . And it was just this "Oh, my God!" And "Ahhh!" And all of a sudden, there was this clarity of a "divine job assignment" that had been named, and there [was] all this liberation to use these gifts. . . . A salient piece of ministry I remember from Jan was her speaking of her experience that when we name gifts, it allows them to flourish.[3]

Cathy Walling
Chena Ridge Friends Meeting, Fairbanks, Alaska

The naming of gifts comes from a place of deep intuition and a keen attunement to Spirit within, amplified by a deep listening and discernment in which the spiritual condition of a person or group can be heard. It also comes from a framework of seeing the world through a spiritual lens, something that can come easily to elders. Thus, elders are often fairly sensitive people, able to notice different energies in a group and in individuals. Some even see physical manifestations of that energy, such as auras or colors. Being intuitive, the elder will often be able to understand what people are hoping to communicate, be able to hear what is under the words. This sensitivity also helps many elders synthesize seemingly disparate ideas or give voice to the sense of the meeting even when others may be confused. Given their sensitivity and intuitiveness, elders have to have done the important inner work that allows them to not be reactive or triggered.

Other characteristics that might flourish in Quaker elders include the following:

- A good understanding of Quaker practice, perhaps some sense of Quaker history, and a grasp of what some call the Quaker "gestalt"—a way of living into our faith that is grounded not in study of the testimonies but in the lived experience of how the Divine is constantly working in and through us.

- A willingness to be vulnerable and open-hearted—vulnerable to God, vulnerable to self, vulnerable to the community. This is a willingness to bare one's deepest self to Spirit and surrender more and more of that self as one is grounded more and more deeply in the Divine, in the mycorrhizae. Mature elders have a healthy, life-giving vulnerability when they recognize and honor boundaries in themselves and in others.

  Most people in our larger culture, including Quakers, have little sense of what is enough and what is hoarding. Transparency is not widely practiced nor encouraged in our Quaker communities. Not having a sense about what is enough and what is hoarding keeps us from being vulnerable because we hide too much. We hide more than we show. We hoard our physical stuff—our insurance, our retirement, and more—most of us Quakers do this hoarding. We do the same with our selves. We hoard our inner selves. This keeps us from a healthy, life-giving vulnerability.

- The characteristics that are found in the best kindergarten teachers. Teachers of young children see the gifts of each of the little beings in their care. They provide the perfect environment for those gifts to flourish and blossom. They don't say no all the time—and when they do, everybody listens.

- An ability to listen deeply, which can be transformative and perhaps even prophetic.

- A willingness to set aside personal concern and comfort, when rightly led, for the good of the person or community or ministry for which they are eldering. This is similar to what some say happens to them in vocal ministry, that they lay themselves aside. Elders lay themselves aside in service of the Spirit and the ministry.

Reflections on Eldering

We all know about prophetic speaking, but prophetic listening means listening to others in such a way that we draw out of them the seeds of their own highest understanding, of their own obedience, of their own vision, that they themselves may not have known were there. Listening can draw forth out of people things that speaking to them cannot.[4]

Elise Boulding, 1920–2010

*****

It should be more than apparent after the things that have been said about what open listening exacts from the listener, why such listeners are scarce and why they are so deeply prized. To "listen" another's soul into a condition of disclosure and discovery may be almost the greatest service that any human being ever performs for another. But in this scrutiny of the business of listening, is that all that has emerged? Is it possible to set forth the perfect listener without a flash of realization that we have been engaged in something more? Is it blasphemous to suggest that over the shoulder of the human listener we have been looking at, there is never absent the silent presence of the Eternal Listener, the living God? For in penetrating to what is involved in listening do we not disclose the thinness of the filament that separates [people] listening openly to one another, and that of God intently listening to each soul?[5]

Douglas V. Steere, 1901–1995

*****

Spiritual Maturity

When Quaker elders mature, they carry within them an integrated blend of authentic humility and spiritual authority, an authority that comes not from knowledge and expertise but from experience of the Spirit. When spiritually mature Quaker elders stand in authentic authority, they become a beacon for the community; they are seen as trustworthy guides. They do not wield power over a community, though they do often seem to embody a true spiritual power that emanates from them into the community. Humility is integrated into mature authority and power. Humility allows us to admit our mistakes, admit we do not know everything, admit that others may know a better way. Spiritual maturity also includes a willingness to be spiritually accountable, even to the point of seeking out those who will be unflinchingly honest. Sometimes, that accountability comes in the form of a care and accountability committee. It may also come in an ongoing relationship with a spiritual director, a spiritual friend, or, most likely, some combination.

When talking about humility, it is important to note the difference between authentic, mature humility and false humility. False humility can come from an unwillingness to acknowledge one's authority and power, which then leads to a lack of accountability. This is quite common in our meetings, where people exercise their power in opaque and deceptive ways because they do not dare own up to it. Power unacknowledged is by definition power abused; it is power masquerading as humility.

Reflection on Eldering

In every Monthly Meeting there is a vital and continuing need for a nucleus of Friends who feel exceptional concern for the deeper spiritual life of the Meeting. They will also feel a concern for the encouragement and guidance of the vocal ministry. These, however, are but the primary qualifications to be looked for in elders. Ideally they need, in addition, a considerable insight into character, an alert spiritual discernment, good judgment, and a fund of ready tact and open friendliness—all of these humbly dedicated to a deeply felt zeal for the spiritual growth of the Society, upheld and purified by the power of constant, watchful prayer. Elders should feel a particular duty to give encouragement and oversight to those who serve in the vocal ministry or public prayer.[6]

—*Faith and Practice* of North Carolina
Yearly Meeting (Conservative), 1983

Among those who are led to the work of eldering, some will be stronger in certain facets than others. One might, for example, have a special gift for grounding worship, while another has a particular aptitude for spiritual nurture. Not surprisingly, no one person has all of these qualities of an elder. Additionally, elders do not materialize fully formed. They must grow into their gifts, and they benefit greatly from more experienced elders nurturing them and from their faithful observance of spiritual disciplines. The spiritual formation of all called into ministry is crucial, knowing that the formation process can happen in many ways seen and hidden.

Although elders often are mature in age as well as in the Spirit, some Quaker spiritual elders are young in years. Signs of being an elder can be seen in children as young as age three, four, or five. The sooner a budding gift is noticed, the more it can be nurtured into its full fruit. Those young ones with a budding gift benefit from being sheltered so that adults who see their gift do not exploit them. Instead, a slow nurturing will allow them to grow even more.

This chapter has focused on qualities that are common in many elders. This list is not exhaustive, and none of these qualities are the final say. Since Spirit works as Spirit will, there are people who do good eldering work and have good fruit even though they do not seem to have any of these qualities.

Queries for Reflection and Discussion

- What are the eldering traits you notice in yourself and in others?

- What might be the temptations or downsides of the characteristics common in elders?

- How have you nurtured eldering traits in yourself and others?

Interlude 3

Noticing Elders

Elaine Emily

Strawberry Creek Friends Meeting, Berkeley, California

What do I see or feel or notice in a person when I say that they're an elder or that they have eldering qualities? Sometimes I see someone and feel a resonance, a feeling, a sense, a knowing that this person is an elder. Others ask all the questions that an elder would. You don't do that if there is not some pull, some something.

When I accompanied a Friend in numerous travels, I was always named as accompanying her in the ministry. Still, most folks hardly saw or acknowledged me. There were always a few, though, who would seek me out and thank me for my service. I always knew that they were fellow elders. They resonated with what I was doing and knew instinctively the power and gift of such spiritual accompaniment.

Of course, most of the people who showed up for workshops that I led were elders. I would always instruct them not to hold the group, nor me, but to participate from a cognitive space. There would always be some who complained that they didn't know how to participate from that place. They habitually held the meeting, group, and minister from a deep place. Some didn't even know that they fell into this place until they were asked not to.

One way I identify a working elder is by the questions they ask. They listen to folks and respond as a "better person" than their usual self. Elders want to know what is happening. When an elder listens with the Spirit, their snippy, whiny, judgmental selves are quieted and the focus becomes listening to the spiritual condition of the other. It is a gift from the Holy Spirit.

Science and spirituality are corroborating each other. Science is documenting that listening and responding from the heart is different from listening and responding from the head. Some folks minister or elder from the headspace. This isn't wrong or bad; still, the ministry is richer and truer when it comes from the heart. Since most of us in the dominant White culture have been taught to value the head response, it often takes some practice to move to the heart's thinking, listening, and knowing place. Elders and ministers need to be able to access both their head and their heart. At their best, eldering and ministering are a dance between the heart and the head, and the heart needs to be in the lead. The mind needs to follow.

I've been present when grade-school children name each other's spiritual gifts. They know who the helpers are. They are the ones who are skilled at listening and can give voice to what the group needs to hear. Teachers of First Day school should be on the lookout for these gifts and help name, nurture, and support these spiritual gifts for the community. I hope that anyone concerned about the future of the Religious Society of Friends will spend time with high school-age Friends. They need to be, and many want to be, called to a higher standard than older Quakers are now offering them.

Chapter 4

The Spiritual Formation of the Elder: Growing in the Gift

Let me say that whosoever undertakes the work of the ministry, not being first reformed themselves, cannot justly expect to be inspired by divine wisdom for the reforming of others by the Word of Truth; for she dwells in holy souls, and makes them friends of God and prophets.[1]

Samuel Bownas, 1676–1753

In the above quote, Samuel Bownas, an early Quaker minister who published a classic book of advice to budding Quaker ministers and elders of his day, writes about the paramount importance of those in ministry "being first reformed themselves." This reformation is the work of spiritual formation. While all Friends, indeed, all people, are invited to the process of spiritual formation, it is particularly necessary—even mandatory—for those, such as elders, who will be nurturing the spiritual formation of others. Because they are involved in the holy work of creating the space and conditions for the spiritual formation of individuals and meeting communities, elders must have some awareness and experience of this path. The path is different for every individual, and it is a lifelong process. Plus, we are all at different places in this nonlinear, even haphazard or meandering, journey of being changed and formed by the Divine.

So, what is spiritual formation? It is the work of the Spirit within freeing a person to become their deepest, truest self and, in doing so, to become more aligned with the Holy.

A nontheist way to think about it is being opened to the Good at the core of life and, being filled with Good and formed to Good, sharing it freely with others.[2] In spiritual formation, elders become more aligned with that which is good and right and more receptive to the good and holy energy that pulses through our days. There is then a growing understanding that the good within us is not for us alone but is to be shared freely among all.

There are several key points to make about spiritual formation and its purpose and fruits. First, it helps us to respond faithfully to the Spirit's call and claim on our lives. Second, we cannot *make* spiritual formation happen to us, but by reading, praying, listening to others, and practicing other spiritual disciplines, we can create fertile ground for the work of the Spirit within. And third, while formation surely edifies us in our relationship with God, its fruits must also be used in service of others.

Spiritual formation releases within us the God-given good and wholeness and holiness with which we are born. This alignment with God and with the good is more complete within us as we continue to turn toward Spirit, living in a way that is ever more attuned to what we may call God's will or, perhaps, the divine dream. The purpose of formation is that we may grow in love for all of Creation.

The formation may be a slow process, and it may be hidden from us. There may also be the equivalent of sudden growth spurts. Sometimes we are formed on a noticeably bumpy path, which may involve finding ourself in the refiner's fire (Malachi 3:2), submitting to the burning away of that which inhibits the fullness of God's Spirit within. It is yielding as clay to the potter's hand. Often it is learning by practice to turn to the Inward Teacher, as George Fox referred to Christ. When we turn to the Inward Teacher for guidance, we find that we see the world in a different light and we manifest more fully the fruit of the Spirit: "love, joy, peace, patience, kindness, generosity, faithfulness, gentleness, and self-control" (Galatians 5:22–23 NRSV). At some points along the way, formation requires us to submit and surrender to a divine impulse beyond our understanding. This surrender is the heart of spiritual formation. When we yield to the work of the Spirit within ourselves, spiritual formation changes how we exist in the world.

How the fruits of formation are used in ministry differs depending on the person and the ministry (see appendix 2 for Elaine's description of her ministry as an elder in non-Quaker settings). Thus, spiritual formation for Quaker elders is an equipping to nurture the spiritual formation of others, both individuals and communities. It is an equipping to live and love more fully.

Spiritual Formation: An Elder's Path

> Like a loving parent, the elder works from her or his own experience of being loved. An elder has lived close to God long enough to have spent time seeing his or her own cleansing, healing and purification. Alone in the quiet and by themselves they've known the nature and marks of God's work and of human struggle. Before learning to discern them in others, they've learned something of where their own resistances and aversions come from before approaching the delicate work of helping or guiding others to the "true north," the Inward Teacher and Guide.[3]
>
> Patricia Loring, 1936–2016

Spiritual formation in the elder begins with the gift that has been given. This formation may begin with the gifts of noticing and nurturing, of groundedness, perhaps a sensitive intuition. For some, the gifts may be given at a young age and exercised throughout their life. Other Friends may grow in a new direction later in life or have the gift noticed later in life. But, at the center of the practice of eldership is something not learned or earned; it is a gift from God, freely bestowed.

An important step in the process is awareness of the gift. This awareness may happen when a youth leader says to a high school Friend, "I notice that others come to you to share their concerns and that you respond with grace and some wisdom." It may be a gradual self-awareness as an adult, noticing that people seem to come to you for insight about their spiritual life. Or, it may be the surprise of being named to a ministry and counsel committee that increases awareness of the gift within. It may be that one is asked to serve on multiple clearness or support committees. The call to eldership often aligns with one's desires and natural tendencies.

This awareness, then, will likely prompt a reflection on what the gift requires of us. Many at this stage may lack the language of "gift from God" or an understanding in a deeper sense that the Divine expects us to use this gift, but for many the awareness will produce a natural desire to engage in actions and behaviors that feel rightly led (even if the language is not there). At this stage of formation, it is good to recognize the need to grow in the gift, especially since the spiritual formation of individuals and communities is a focus of elders. It is a time of learning, and most will probably decline to involve themselves in some of the more challenging situations of eldering.

The path of spiritual formation looks different for each individual, depending on the unique qualities of the person and the way the gift is manifest in them. It may also depend on whether there is an experienced and willing elder to notice the budding gift and to be a mentor. A new elder's formation is also affected by the readings that fall into their hands and the experiences that come their way. A major part of what happens in the formation process is that elders learn how to listen to their inner self—the Inward Teacher.

Along the way, it is likely that an elder will encounter situations they are not prepared for and they will feel bruised, confused, and discouraged. That is when we need each other. It is useful for a Friend in these circumstances to have an experienced elder to consult with as they perhaps ask, "Was there something I could have said or done differently?" Or, someone to simply hold their hand and say, "Yes, sometimes it's really hard." Eldering may be hard because the Spirit is using the elder vigorously. It may be hard because of a steep learning curve. It may be hard to witness how poorly Quakers can behave with each other. It may be hard because the Adversary is at work. The companionship and prayer of a seasoned elder can be a great help in guiding a new elder along the path of spiritual formation.

Elders need to take responsibility for those elders coming up and accompany them. And, they should never assume that they are so spiritually grounded or spiritually astute that they can do this work without being continually taught and nurtured. This is part of accountability—checking in with and accompanying each other as elders. Eldering, like everything Quaker, is a communal thing. It's not individualistic.

The process of spiritual formation is often winding and sometimes painful since it requires dying to the false self in order to be reborn into the true self. Through the process, we are inevitably brought to a deeper and broader faith and to the right use of our God-given spiritual gifts. This formation process has no beginning and no ending. It may seem like we begin again many times, which makes sense. We always have more to learn. The goal is not perfection. In fact, there really is no goal. Rather, as we submit to spiritual formation and to God, there is an increasingly abundant harvest of the fruit of the Spirit. Samuel Bownas wrote the following of ministers; it also applies to those in the ministry of eldership:

> There must be a state of sanctification (in degree) known, by the spirit of judgment and burning, before any can be proper objects to be receivers of this inspiring gift, that can only assist a minister and make [them] instrumental of doing good to others. The tree must be good before the fruit can be so; and right and true ministers are to be known by their fruits. This being granted, which I think can't be denied, then it follows that none, without being thus qualified, can be called to the work of the ministry by a divine inspiration of the Holy Spirit.[4]

Samuel Bownas, 1676–1753

In any kind of spiritual work of ministers or elders, a prerequisite of being faithful to the Spirit is paying attention to your body, paying attention more and more until you know what your body is saying to you. You have to at least dip your toe into the knowing of your body's language before you can ever start accompanying other people who are dipping their toe into this knowing. This body language and body knowing is becoming more common and accepted, even among academics, than it was in the 1990s. Attending to the body is something that many elders do naturally; it is a quality of many elders. In addition, the process of getting to know one's body is part of an elder's spiritual formation. All of us, not just elders, need to do this work so that our body awareness becomes more present and more pronounced than it would be if we didn't do this work. Spirit can talk to and inform us through our body. What happens in the body bypasses our consciousness and its limitations.

For as Long as You Shall Live

Spiritual formation is indeed a lifelong process of increasing surrender of our life to Spirit on the path to becoming more fully aligned with and faithful to God and to our best selves. It is an integrated process involving body, heart, and mind. It is an integrative process that brings all our disparate parts into a unified whole. It is not linear. There are many steps forward, backward, sideways, and even in circles— and sometimes a spiral up or down. The prayer is that, whatever the direction, spiritual formation is always moving toward greater submission to and alignment with a God eager for us to be all of who we are.

To put it in traditional Quaker and Christian terms, this is about being crucified; there are things in us that need to die before we are able to be born again into the whole and holy people we are created to be. We need to surrender, to submit. We say, "Thy will, not mine." Or, less and less of me and more and more of Spirit. Or, we become more ourself, our fullest self, not less. Rather than being cut off from who we are and who we are created to be, we must die to our false self, as many spiritual teachers say, so that we can live our true self with whole-hearted abundance.

In other words, surrender, obedience, and submission are at the core of spiritual formation. The process of physical, emotional, psychological, mental, spiritual, and whole-life work leads to spiritual maturity and a mature exercise of the gift of eldering. This does not necessarily mean that we wait until we are perfectly prepared to exercise the gift because, of course, there is no perfection. It may mean we need to step back for a time from eldering to submit more fully to the formation process. Often, it means that we are formed as we do the work. We do a piece of ministry, and we learn, each and every time, as we keep our hearts soft and teachable.

This self-emptying path of surrender and submission looks different for each of us. Some people seem to be asked to surrender more than others. It may even be true that, for some, the path of surrender may in fact be a path toward assertiveness. As with so much of the formation process, discernment is key. We need to discern on ever deeper levels who or what to submit to and when and how to surrender. Whatever the individual path of surrender may be, it is a whole-mind and whole-body process.

This surrender takes place in the different facets that make us into a whole. The following sections address these separately to aid in understanding, but there are overlaps and blurred lines between each of these areas of surrender.

Surrender of Our Intellect

Quakerism is a spiritually mature religion because the body, the congregation, finds the spiritual way forward together. No doctrine or creed gives us the absolute answer. In this way, Quakerism is demanding of its members. The intellect needs to be surrendered to Spirit and engaged in the process of discerning the way forward. It is neither totally rational nor nonrational. Grounded in worship, all our different intelligences are called forward. The intellect brings together knowledge of the political, social, scientific, and economic landscape that we all live in.

Elders need to surrender their intellect to the Holy One and seek divine guidance in how to nurture and use their intelligence. For some elders, that leads to knowing gospel order and Quaker history. For others, it may mean the ability to creatively weave different threads and ideas together into a whole that moves individuals or groups toward God. It might also be seen in a treasurer who is not bound by the idea of scarcity but who sees money as a resource for the community to use to the highest good. All of these may be using their intellect in the manner of elders.

Reflection on Eldering

How do we use our intellect as elders? We can be in an eldering role holding a gathered body, and words are being spoken and we are able to be with words and to be with the "with." In the gathered body, as a whole, an elder's mind becomes elastic, it becomes expanded so that it can hold the words as they come, however they come: words spoken in kindness, in conflict, in prayer. They are all held in the mind; the mind seems to become more elastic to hold them. This elasticity doesn't end when the eldering period is passed. It is part of the expanded mind, the expanded mental capacity that happens as you deepen in your practice as an elder.

As you deepen, you're able to hold what you couldn't hold before. In the past, you divided things into "this was okay, but this was not okay; this was the beginning, this was not." The practice of eldering can lead to a sense in the moment of timelessness. A sinking down into spaciousness. There is a sense of the body dropping down, dropping away, and of the mind opening, expanding.

Dorothy Henderson
Grass Valley Friends Meeting, California

Psychological Surrender

Each elder needs to become self-aware enough that they don't project their own thoughts, feelings, emotions, beliefs, wounds, and ideas onto others. This is the major work of psychological surrender, a giving over of one's past and inner workings and how they affect current behavior. Of course, this is a lifelong pursuit; it is vital in knowing that which is mine and that which is not, to know what is being given to me by the Divine and what is my own good idea or what instead may be unprocessed trauma or psychological dings.

Many of us have deep wounds that may never be fully healed. Often, those deep wounds are what make us more aware and compassionate and allow us to be helpful to others. However, if the wounds are not tended to, they can lead to the creation of more wounds to self and others. Therefore, it is our own great responsibility to know those wounds and find others to hold us accountable to tending them while opening to the Divine Guide. Sometimes this seems contradictory, and sometimes it transforms into paradox. Psychotherapy for both ministers and elders is sometimes helpful, possibly mandatory, to be able to release the fullness of our gifts to our community. Many kinds of therapy and other practices, such as twelve-step groups or yoga, are widely available to add to and enhance our Quaker practices. Clearness committees, faithfulness groups, anchor or spiritual accountability committees, and spiritual friendships all can be part of our healing into the fullness of our gifts. While this is work every member of the meeting needs to pay attention to, it is especially important for those called to eldering because of the often intimate, one-on-one work many elders do.

The process of submitting and surrendering psychologically is primarily about the transformation of the ego, or perhaps the redemption of the ego. Some say the ego must be subdued or diminished. Instead, our belief is that, as a core part of our identity, the ego must be brought into service of our higher power, our best self. Sometimes, Friends are hyperfocused on their ego and have a hard time knowing the difference between their ego and what is beyond ego. In waiting worship and other meditation practices, we offer our ego to the process of spiritual formation, consenting to its transformation. Early Quakers wrote often about being changed men and women. Isaac Penington exhorts us to "give over thine own willing."[5] This seems to point to the necessity of ego transformation as we mature and are formed. One other point about ego is that most people who are worried about their ego probably don't need to be. Those who are not worried about their ego probably should be more concerned.

Emotional Surrender

Emotions are another gift from God in need of attention, very closely tied to the psychological work. Emotions can be a powerful force for change if they are tethered; unharnessed, emotions can bring a destructive energy.

Many practices have us notice our emotions as they rise and fall. Learning to know your own relationship to your emotions as they interact with and inform your spiritual gifts is important. Are you being triggered by some past trauma? Are you responding in real time to a current situation? Many elders pick up others' emotions or are able to "read" emotions in others. This is a wonderful gift when it is "clean," that is, when it is not complicated by the elder's own emotional needs and history. Our meetings very likely have members who bring some not-yet-resolved trauma that sows confusion in the community. The more emotionally mature and grounded the elder is, the better they see these behaviors for what they are and are of service to the individual and the community.

If we are gifted with being able to "read" or "experience" others' emotions, we need also to learn, when we accompany a person, how to let those emotions come and pass through us so that we don't carry them. In other words, it is important to have good boundaries. We may learn this through firsthand experience, psychotherapy, or in our accountability relationships. But learn it we must, and that begins with a willingness to surrender our emotional selves into the care of the Divine Mother. This surrender is where we begin to loosen our hold on our emotions as the driver. It is where we can both fully feel our feelings and have enough space to explore and query our emotions in order to learn from them. It means knowing which are our own emotions and which are the ones we are picking up from others. It means, also, that we know ourselves well enough to take a time-out when we are flooded with emotions that distort our view. This is similar to pulling over in a hard rain until it eases up and we can again drive safely.

Spiritual Surrender

To "give over thine own willing," in Isaac Penington's words, is one of the simplest ways to understand spiritual surrender. It is a giving over of our spiritual willfulness, our sense that we know what is needed and, by God, we're going to do it! Another way of understanding spiritual surrender comes in the first three steps of Alcoholics Anonymous:

1. We admitted we were powerless over alcohol—that our lives had become unmanageable.

2. Came to believe that a Power greater than ourselves could restore us to sanity.

3. Made a decision to turn our will and our lives over to the care of God as we understood Him.

For those in AA, the focus is, of course, on alcohol addiction. Still, those first three steps are the path to spiritual surrender, which is the yielding of one's spirit to the Spirit. It is yielding to something bigger than oneself.

There are many spiritual practices that serve us in the discipline of spiritual surrender. Of course, no one practice is best for every person at every time. It is important to discern here what practices Spirit may be inviting you to. Quakers have traditionally talked about daily retirement, Scripture reading, lectio divina, waiting worship, spiritual friendships, and accountability committees as disciplines that are helpful in surrender.

One of Quakers' core spiritual practices, sitting in silent or "waiting" worship, is foundational in teaching spiritual surrender because it is through worship and meditation that we learn internally the motion of surrender and how to discern God's voice from others. As we sit in the sacred silence, we may become more able to still our minds and learn not to run with every thought that randomly pops into our awareness. This spiritual practice may take years to master, and even then, we may return to the beginning over and over again.

Reflections on Eldering

While discussion of sin differs significantly throughout the various branches of the Religious Society of Friends today, there is no doubt that it was a significant point of discussion in the early years of the Quaker movement. The concept of "the Seed of Christ" is sometimes still heard today, but far less frequently do we discuss the idea that there are, in fact, two seeds we ought to pay attention to.

As I understand it, the way early Friends understood the situation was that the Seed of Christ is an inherent and eternal part of what it means to be a human. It was available to every single person regardless of their beliefs, professed religion, or previous actions; the Seed of God was a permanent feature of being human. Conversely, the Seed of the Serpent was something that could be cast out and was not an inherent part of humanity's nature. The tricky part is that though it was possible to cast out the Seed of the Serpent, it would eventually—sneakily!—return.

Sinking down into the Seed of Christ is the same kind of holy practice that helps to cast out the Seed of the Serpent anew.

Callid Keefe-Perry
Three Rivers Worship Group, Fresh Pond Monthly
Meeting, Cambridge, Massachusetts

Eventually, when our minds are still and clear enough, spiritual surrender leads to a deepening transformation. As part of this path, there may come exhilarating mountaintop experiences. There will also be the painful encounters with self as the ego loses its grip and becomes transformed. This is a never-ending process, and elders will always have need of eldering companions who can accompany them as they traverse this terrain. For some, it may take focused prayer and searching to find the right companions for this journey. Those companions may change over time.

Physical Surrender

When we talk about physical surrender as part of spiritual formation, we mean bringing our physical selves, as temples of the Holy Spirit, into alignment with the Holy. Quakerism is well documented as a very physical spirituality. We are called Quakers, after all, because we "quake"—or, at least, some of us do. Some of the discernment around whether we are being led to minister in meeting for worship is rooted in the physical: heart racing or pounding, feeling cold or heat, tears, and other manifestations. Also related to the physical, we talk about "the body," meaning the gathered assembly of worshippers. Some call this "the body of Christ," and as a body we are asked to surrender as much as we are asked to do so as individuals. For many elders, physical surrender supports the work of eldering.

The Christian tradition, from which Quakerism sprouted, has many examples of people who physically submit to Spirit. Mary in the Gospel stories, when she says yes to being the Mother of God. Jesus, when he says before his crucifixion—his death by torture, "My Father, if this cannot pass unless I drink it, your will be done" (Matthew 26:42 NRSV). Friend Tom

Fox, a member of the Christian Peacemaker Teams in Iraq, put his body in harm's way and was killed.[6] A lot of Quakers participate in civil disobedience that puts them in physically dangerous situations. While not all are asked to submit to events as extreme as these, there are many ways that elders may be asked to physically submit to Spirit. For example, the practice of yoga, qigong, or tai chi may be asked of elders as a way to prepare their bodies to be vessels of the Holy One, to be bearers of God.

Reflections on Eldering

In the summer of 2018 I was called to be an elder for the clerk of our yearly meeting, a three-year commitment. At that time, I had a daily yoga practice, and in the spring of 2019 I added a daily qi gong practice. Over time, I had a sense of yoga as being about the "me" and qi gong as about the "not me." These two practices transformed my practice of eldering. They contributed to my awareness of my body when eldering so that physically my body became more attuned to the "me" and the "not me."

Or perhaps eldering transformed my practice of yoga and qi gong. As an elder, the teachings of the body became more available to me. I began to experience my body calling me to actions, to move or not move. The physical became a part of the practice of eldering. The physical manifested in the spiritual, and the spiritual manifested in the physical.

Ultimately, the eldering has become a practice of the body and the spirit. They are not separate. It has deepened my experience of Penington's words, "Nothing found in me but Christ, and me found nowhere but in Christ." In moments of eldering, the "me" and the "not me" become not separate. No inner and outer. Just Christ.

Dorothy Henderson
Grass Valley Friends Meeting, California

*****

[When traveling in the ministry in Australia with Elaine Emily,] I was mindful of the need for daily walks to continue to tend the physical body while doing this spiritual work. At various times the physical act of walking would move energy, clear our heads, and assist with discernment. We ended up walking each afternoon and sometimes in the evening as well. We called these times together our 'discernment walks.'[7]

Cathy Walling
Chena Ridge Friends Meeting, Fairbanks, Alaska

We sometimes talk about the heart-brain or gut-brain connection. Often our bodies know things before our brains can find words or constructs for why we feel funny, or our chest is tight, or the hairs on the back of our neck are standing up. Taking the time to figure out what your body is saying is important for many elders. Although it's hard to put into words, elders are informed by attending to the feelings or knowings in their bodies. In a similar way, others may feel something from the presence of an elder that they also have a hard time articulating.

Reflection on Eldering

After I had been recorded as a minister, I was especially glad to have an occasional opportunity with Rachel Livezey, whom I once embarrassed by calling a "true elder." More than once, after we had sat together in a living silence, I would be moved to ask a question and discover that, even as I spoke the words, I would know the answer! My explanation for this is that a gifted elder is so "clear" in her own spirit that when she is really "present" to another person, that person's mind also becomes clearer, making it easier to discern the truth. Rachel also "knew" things about me, about my trials and temptations and weaknesses, without my telling her—and I know that she prayed fervently for me.[8]

William Taber (1927–2005)

This attending to our internal experiences means that we are taking the time and are practicing to get to know our instrument, the instrument that the Holy Spirit uses to

49

communicate with us and through us. Listening with our bodies to the Holy One while simultaneously listening to another person or group takes practice. The more we practice, the more skilled we become.

The practice of surrendering our physical selves to the Divine Good may begin with taking up a yoga practice or a change in diet, such as abstaining from sugar, caffeine, or alcohol. Such decisions may come through a revelation that our physical activities and what we eat and drink affect us spiritually and interpersonally. In that way, body-based practices can help connect mind and body. Yoga, which means union, is a path toward mind-body integration. The asanas (body postures) are designed to discipline the body so it can learn how to be still and invite the mind into stillness. Qigong and tai chi teach us how to work with energy to ground and center our beingness. Though some of our modern practices might have been foreign to early Quakers, getting to know our bodies and listening to what they tell us has long been a Quaker tradition.

Reflections on Eldering

Talking about the cross, my experience is having spent some time leaning against an oak tree and feeling that when I stood up there was a cross of oak in my body and I carried it around for a time. It was a time of engaging with a lot of old, messy conflicts in meetings (and in my work life). At some point, it was like the cross left me, the crucified Christ left me, and went way up into the night sky. And a little star came down and landed in the place on the opposite side of my heart. That was my soul place, very sweet but strange. It was not something that I talked about a lot, then or now. I felt empowered by it, changed by it, but it is not something I could understand rationally.

Anonymous

Surrender of Habits

When it comes to submission and surrender, it is really all of our life that needs to eventually be turned over to God: our refrigerator, car, bank account, and bed; what we eat; where we spend our time and how we get there; how we spend our money; and our intimate relationships. As we mature spiritually, more of our life will be surrendered and aligned with Spirit. This evolution happens best in the context of an accountability group. If surrender is not happening in the context of community, it is all too easy to keep nice and tidy in the abstract, to look right and say the right things without letting God disturb our "perfect" garden. This spiritual stuff becomes far more real when we bring all of life into the gaze of an accountability partner or committee.

An accountability committee may, for example, help a minister to tend more faithfully to their finances, enabling them to then be more faithful in their call to ministry. Elders sometimes address accountability issues related to addiction or personal integrity (see appendix 3).

Reflections on Eldering

Finally, there is the old and basic problem of sin. In this case, sin means clinging to old habits that are no longer acceptable, putting our love for these old habits before our love for Christ who is leading us into a new way of life. I am not referring to habits that are themselves sinful, because they should be dealt with irrespective of any emerging spiritual gifts; I am referring to habits that are innocuous of themselves, but that hamper or interfere with the new gift. These must be dealt with in order to make room for God's developing plan for our life. . . . Consecrating our lives to our gifts, and developing the individual and group disciplines that enable us to exercise and receive the fruits of our communities' giftedness, take time to learn and practice. It is the mercy of God, therefore, to bestow the seed of a gift, allowing it to grow and come to maturity in our lives, as we learn to care for it and prepare for its maturity.[9]

Lloyd Lee Wilson
Friendship Friends Meeting,
Greensboro, North Carolina

Although some Quakers chafe at the idea of accountability, it is a key foundational piece for any form of ministry, including eldering. Without it, elders may drift into thinking that they know everything about what is good and right and best—or that they ought to. This is a form of "persistent sinfulness" that may do grave damage to a community. A network of accountability can help elders see more clearly how their own motives may be entangled in God's authentic leading. When elders submit to a committee or some other structure of accountability—and through this, submit to Spirit—they are more likely to be ever more deeply grounded in love as the impetus for the work that is laid on their heart, even the most difficult of this work. And, if we are not growing in love, we must ask—are we truly in a process of spiritual formation? Are we truly elders?[10]

Sharing with another the ways that we have fallen short in our personal relations and our relationship with God, which some would call confession, needs to be part of an accountability relationship. One of the reasons twelve-step work has proven so valuable to many is the accountability and confessional component. If we keep parts of ourselves and what we do hidden, if we never bring to light the ways we err and fall short, we never open up to the fullness of God in our lives; we hold back and avoid the opportunity to be washed clean, to be made new and whole. None of us wants to expose our worst self to others, and yet when we do, it frees us to move forward.

Reflection on Eldering

> We travel often in a dark country, and that darkness clings to our souls, our minds, our hearts, and our bodies. The pain that we feel can cause us to lash out at others, or scare them, or indict them. We have to do our own work of confession, grieving, contrition, forgiveness, healing, and repentance over and over again. This is not solitary work.
>
> Carl Magruder
> Strawberry Creek Friends Meeting, Berkeley, California

The following is an excerpt from a conversation between Angela York Crane (Chester Friends Meeting, Pennsylvania) and Elaine Emily about eldering in 2017 or 2018. They speak, among other things, to the need for communal recognition of and accountability for elders.

Angela: I'm ambivalent about eldering. One of the facets is I don't know if my ability to elder comes from health in me or from a place of ill health, hypervigilance. I am not clear about where my gifts of eldering come from. Is there something I could be aware of to be more whole with them, a way to see if I can discern and separate what is the hypervigilance that I learned and needed as a child and what is discernment of the Spirit? I need to be very present to where the life in me for eldering is coming from.

Secondly, I don't know that the Religious Society of Friends accepts that eldering is part of our practice and that it's important. I don't know that elders are given their due. Certainly, ministers—those who use elders—understand the importance of elders, but the majority of the body doesn't get [understand] or support elders/eldering. In a sense, elders do what they do, but they're also neutered. It's like we're told to elder with our hands tied behind our back, with our awareness kept internal rather than being expressed outwardly.

Because there is ambivalence, and because we elder invisibly and with our gifts tied up, there's not much accountability. I don't know what accountability for an elder would look like, but there isn't any—I know that. We should be accountable to the body, but since the body doesn't accept or understand the work we do, there's no mutuality or accountability body to body, body to people. A lot of people do introduce the elders, and that is kind of a way to make them accountable to the body, to the people present. That sometimes feels like it's just lip service. It feels very unmoored.

So, I wonder: What would it look like to ask for buy-in? Can the elder actually elder here? What would it look like to ask permission or consent from the body—to have them say, "We will be eldered"? Both the elder and the body need to submit and surrender; they need to consent to that.

Elaine: I think a lot of eldering has close similarities to the Alcoholics Anonymous model, specifically when it comes to enabling and co-dependency. Some elders might also inappropriately insert themselves into situations because of their need to be needed—a co-dependent characteristic.

An elder who is not spiritually grounded can become an enabler of ungrounded ministry. When this happens, the eldering is not conscious and is not explicitly consensual. It's habitual, not conscious. Yet I have skills and gifts that I learned as a child growing up in a dysfunctional, though not alcoholic, family. For me, the difference now is that when I elder, it is consensual. It's very explicit, and it is consensual. It uses the same skills as in dysfunctional relationships but in a very different framework. Not only is it consensual, it is time-limited. That means that I, and these elder gifts, are not available to just anyone, anytime.[11]

Spiritual Formation and Shadow Work

Now, Friends, deal plainly with yourselves, and let the eternal Light search you, and try you, for the good of your souls. For this will deal plainly with you. It will rip you up, and lay you open, and make all manifest which lodges in you; the secret subtlety of the enemy of your souls, this eternal searcher and trier will make manifest. Therefore all to this come, and by this be searched, and judged, and led and guided. For to this you must stand or fall.[12]

Margaret Fell, 1614–1702

The moral man is he who is opposed to injustice per se, opposed to injustice wherever he finds it; the moral man looks for injustice first of all in himself.[13]

Bayard Rustin, 1912–1987

Some of the most important work the Inward Christ does in us has to do with what Carl Jung, a psychiatrist and psychoanalyst, called bringing into awareness our shadow self. There is a lot written about shadow work elsewhere. Our brief touch on it here should in no way minimize its importance.

One way of describing shadow work is by talking about people's blind spots, the things we don't see, or don't want to see, about ourselves, the parts of ourselves our experiences that we have split off into unconsciousness. Those things submerged in the shadows are sometimes what we perceive as our ugly, shameful parts. Sometimes, though, they are what Jung called the golden shadow, the best parts of who a person is. The shadow contains energy, life force, that is not available for our life until it comes into consciousness. It may be thought of as what lies in the fertile fungi or deep in the shadows of the forest.

What comes from the shadows may be unconscious and yet still very intentional. For example, someone might very intentionally say something hurtful to a fellow meeting member yet have no understanding that it may be coming from something buried deep within themselves rather than from the issue at hand. Likewise, the work White Quakers of European descent need to do around race and decolonization has much hidden in the shadows. Until that is brought into the light, into consciousness, the behavior of these Quakers will likely continue to do harm. Jung consistently stated that until the unconscious becomes conscious, the unconscious is the driver. Paul stated the same: "I do not understand my own actions. For I do not do what I want, but I do the very thing I hate" (Romans 7:15 NRSV). Shadow work is bringing the unconscious into consciousness so that we can have more choice about what we say and do and how we say and do it.[14]

Whether golden or shameful, these shadow parts are rejected or denied for many different reasons. Unless and until they are brought into awareness and addressed, they heavily influence our thoughts and behaviors. This is true for elders and for others in the meeting. Elders have the responsibility to work with their own shadows. When they do that work, they also may be helpful in bringing to awareness other shadow forces that are at work within a meeting or an individual.

For those called into the ministry of eldering, tending to the shadows is a must to keep the work we do as clean and fruitful as possible. We pray for the grace to see what is in the shadows and the grace and guidance to then do our inner work with our shadow beings and influences. It should be no surprise if this involves therapy; if something is in our shadow spaces, it may well be there because we needed it to be there at some earlier point in our life that now needs attention. When we ignore what is in our shadows, that stuff leaks out, sometimes in harmful, dangerous ways.

Reflection on Eldering

When we act out of loneliness our actions easily become violent. The tragedy is that much violence comes from a demand for love. When loneliness drives our search for love, kissing easily leads to biting, caressing to hitting, looking tenderly to looking suspiciously, listening to overhearing, and surrender to rape. The human heart yearns for love: love without conditions, limitations, or restrictions. But no human being is capable of offering such love, and each time we demand it we set ourselves on the road to violence.

How then can we live nonviolent lives? We must start by realizing that our restless hearts, yearning for perfect love, can only find that love through communion with the One who created them.[15]

Henri Nouwen, 1932–1996

The Importance of Soul Work

Remember: the spiritual formation of elders is important because elders are involved in the spiritual formation of others. This ongoing work does not necessarily get easier. Yet it is soul work, the work of transformation, and that can bring elders great joy. It is a most important journey, this path of spiritual formation. Because it is a life-long process, you don't one day get a degree that says, "You are fully formed." Be assured that each of us involved in this project can tell stories about times when we fell short, times when we were willful, times when grace rescued us, and times when an unlikely person said something that opened up a new window into understanding the Divine and seeing more clearly how we are called to serve.

The mystery and grace of spiritual formation is that it is way beyond our control. We can do things that might open us more to being formed, but it is God who does the forming, regardless of what we do. Our task is to enter the darkness, embrace whatever is there, bring it into the light, hold it in mindfulness, and forgive everything.[16]

Queries for Reflection and Discussion

- What in your life has been especially spiritually formative for you?

- What is your relationship with surrender, and how has that formed you spiritually?

Interlude 4

How the Call to Eldership Grew in an Individual Called Later in Life

Dinah Bachrach
Redwood Forest Friends Meeting, Santa Rosa, California

Stage 1: What, me, an elder? Not me!

The first time Elaine Emily casually asked me if I might be interested in eldering, I felt clearly, "No way. She doesn't know me. I am not only fairly new to Quakers, only became a member about four years ago, but I continue to feel inadequate in the spiritual department. My parents were Communists in my early years, firmly anti-Christian and anything spiritual."

All my life, I have been drawn to relationship, to deep connections with people. Becoming a therapist felt natural to me. I still feel it's a blessing to be able to make my living being intimate with people and helping them value their innate goodness. As I opened my mind and heart to exploring myself as a spiritual being, I realized that what I had deemed psychological was in fact spiritual. My deepest belief has always been in the goodness in people, buried though it might be. It was not a big leap for me to take an "o" out of Good to the notion that there is that of God in everyone. Like many, I prefer the nongendered, nonpersonal word Spirit to the word God, but I can easily transpose now.

Still, I struggle with imposter syndrome and have to struggle against my self-doubts and judgments and comparisons with other Friends whom I admire for their depth of worship, their personal relationship with God or Jesus, their mystical experiences, etc. I must continually come back to what I am, what I experience, what others may recognize in me that I deny.

Interlude 4: How the Call to Eldership Grew

When I look back, I now recall a few instances that held spiritual power for me: feeling a sudden oneness with others breathing together; hearing a reassuring phrase in a moment of anguish, once coming from inside my body and once from a tree: and, at the end of a three-day solo vision quest in the wilderness, I felt a strong message from the trees that I should become an antinuclear activist to protect them. Recently, when I participated in an eldering workshop led by Gordon Bishop, he gave us four minutes to Go Find God! and to my surprise I did, in the blazing Japanese maple tree outside my window.

Stage 2: Being tapped for an unusual eldering job at my yearly meeting: "Well, okay, I'll try . . ."

Dorothy Henderson, one of those Friends whose Christian spiritual life is front and center and who is doing some heavy-duty eldering herself, asked me if I would elder for a young woman who would be handling all the Zoom technology for our first virtual yearly meeting session. She said that she and others on the Eldering Sub-Committee thought I had the makings of an elder. I felt honored and unsure but willing to learn and see what I might be able to offer. As I began to meet with this woman, also a newish Quaker who had never had an elder but was very open to me, I discovered that I could blend my deep familiarity with attuning to another as a therapist with that deeper sense of Spirit I felt with trees when we worshipped a little together. We both began to feel good and close from these meetings.

Then, once during a yearly meeting session, as she was doing her work ushering people in with Zoom, I observed her doing a common White person micro-aggression to a person of color. I wrestled internally and asked for guidance from the eldering group. Was it part of eldering to speak with her about this, or was it coming from my activist self? I got support that I should follow my instincts, which might be coming from Spirit, and just share my inner experience with her. I did, and she was open and grateful.

Stage 3: Things escalate.

Dorothy invited me to be part of the yearly meeting's Eldering Sub-Committee, and although I felt like a "junior" elder, I accepted because I knew, liked, and respected several others on the committee. The thought in me was, "What do they see in me that I don't?" I stayed in the background and learned more about how each of them experienced being an elder, no two the same, the challenges they encountered as they worked internally and within the relationship to support Spirit in the other, the minister.

A few months later, a friend who had been nominated to be the yearly meeting's rising clerk called me out of the blue to tell me that she was considering me as a possible elder for her. Would I be open to that? I was surprised and honored, and I agreed to explore this with her. She had another person or two she was considering, so we kept meeting and talking for a couple of months. During this time, I had to really do battle internally between the voice that said, "You are fooling them; you don't know how to do this thing called deep worship" and the voice that said, "These people do connect with Spirit and they sense this in you. Have faith; you are being called. Remember when and how you have felt imbued with Spirit." The doubting voice was stronger, and I needed to talk it through.

I called Dorothy, who is unfailingly honest and real. She listened to all my doubts and fears, reiterated that all on the committee felt my gifts, and said that she saw me as having two essential elder qualities: a deep listener and a spiritual seeker. These felt true. Seeker, yes. I have been on a spiritual journey since my vision quest at age thirty-three. I have been working at meditating daily, mostly with a Thich Nhat Hanh gatha (a Buddhist practice), though I've tried many other ways. Trees and music open inner doors for me. When I focus on another person and attune to their core, I feel very centered, unaware of myself but trusting what comes to me to say or do. Dorothy's words calmed me and gave me the courage to talk honestly with my friend the rising clerk about both my insecurities and my securities as an elder. After a time, she became clear she wanted to have me as her elder. Who knows how this will unfold? I continue to feel insecure at times. The two voices continue their debate, but my confidence that in fact there is that of God in me and that others see it sometimes when I can't or won't is growing.

Interlude 4: How the Call to Eldership Grew

Just recently, when Elaine Emily called to ask me to write this vignette, I explained firmly that I don't have mystical experiences, etc., and then at some point told her about my vision quest connection with the trees and the direction I felt to become an activist to protect them. She laughed and said, "And you don't think that was a mystical experience?" So, what do I know? Not much, but seeking isn't about knowledge.

Interlude 5

Physical Experiences of Eldering

Elaine Emily
Strawberry Creek Friends Meeting, Berkeley, California

There are physical aspects to eldering, and I will try to address all that I can think of. As I was learning to accompany a piece of ministry, the first sensation I remember is of the inner voice leading me to call or accept an invitation. You might question whether this is a physical experience. Of course, I didn't hear with my physical ears, and yet it seemed as though I did. There was and is an internal physical sensation when something is on my plate. A sensation in my core dantian (energy center) is every bit as physical as when someone says, metaphorically, "It was like getting kicked in the gut." If you have had this experience, you actually feel it.

Learning to notice and accept these sensations was a large part of succumbing to eldering for me. When I first accompanied a minister in a large group, I would sink into the deepest, most wonderful worship I'd ever experienced. I would sit almost motionless for long periods of time, three to four hours at a stretch. Our physical bodies are not meant to not move. So, while the motionless worship felt amazing spiritually, my physical body needed significant recovery time. I would have to take time to "come up" to normal social interactions and adjust to the harshness of those everyday social interactions. Likewise, my physical body needed time to recover as well.

As I worked with more elders holding the minister, I would not descend as deep nor come up as disconnected from my body. It seems to me that when a piece of ministry that is being given by someone is particularly true to the Spirit, I quake, a very physical movement of my body that doesn't feel initiated by my physical being.

Interlude 5: Physical Experiences of Eldering

From time to time, I've been led to either sit in a particular place, move to sit closer to someone, or move farther away. Sometimes these nudges make sense to my rational mind, and sometimes the reason remains a mystery. Sometimes I wonder if I'm just making the nudge up. I'll never really know, though there have been enough affirmations to keep me listening and obeying. Being intensely focused on the minute or being open to the much larger, diffuse focus registers differently in my body. It's like the difference in looking at something up close, trying to get my eyes to see better than they do, and looking with my eyes closed and gathering impressions. My body tenses and relaxes in different ways, ways that take attention to notice.

Early on in my eldering work, I would be so filled with energy that I would need to do something physical to dissipate the energy, like running, walking, giving a massage, or doing energy work for someone. At the other end of the scale, after traveling in the ministry for days, weeks, or months, upon returning home I needed to cocoon, to just vegetate. Thinking, planning, or executing movement beyond the most elementary tasks was out of my range of capacity. I would often cry, without emotion or for any reason I could discern other than for being emptied and cleansed.

Other physical manifestations of eldering can run the whole gamut from digestive upset, being hot or cold, headaches, pains, itching, and so forth. Quaking is one of these manifestations.

I started quaking long before I met Quakers. It wasn't gentle. I had been going to hear a medicine man talk. My experience of him was often that he was speaking directly to me. A question would form in my mind, and as it would form he would begin to answer it. One of the things he described is how the Spirit would come at night and "have its way with him," and once he quaked so badly that he broke the bed. He was a big man. So, when I started quaking, I understood two things. I understood that it was the Holy Spirit and that it was Kundalini (divine feminine energy) somehow, and that was a good thing even though it was strange and weird. I really wanted to sweat with that man, and you can't sweat if you're bleeding. He would have sweats every two weeks and I would bleed every two weeks for a very long time until I decided that I probably wasn't supposed to sweat with him.

The quaking didn't feel at all like it was generated by me. It came in meditation, too. I was involved with a man at the time. We did a lot of meditation together. The quaking happened to me a lot during sex. He was like, "Oh, my gosh. Should I be calling 911?"

In those days, I would be awakened in the middle of the night, every night, to get up and meditate, and quaking would often be a part of that. When I was going to sleep, I would often experience a period of quaking.

In addition to quaking, when I first came to Orange Grove Friends Meeting in Pasadena, California, I also wept a lot. Orange Grove had two doors off the library. They had a front door, too, but the two doors off the library had been for the men's side and the women's side of the meetinghouse, though that was no longer how the doors were used. I would come in what had been the men's side and sit right next to the door. And I would weep. There would be tears, tears, tears. And when meeting for worship was up, I would leave because I was not ready to enter into normal social discourse. Those tears, like the quaking, were also an expression of the Spirit.

Chapter 5

Care for the Meeting as a Body Gathered by God: The Work of the Elder

The Covenant Community

Our Quaker meetings are, at their best and most mature and most spiritually grounded, covenant communities where people are committed to each other in a sacred web of relationship with each other and with God. While the word "covenant" is not usually used in our times, early Quakers did use it to describe their communal relationship in the Spirit, as Friend Sandra Cronk and others describe. Additionally, as Cronk writes: "Covenant is a theme which pervades the entire Scripture. The dictionary definition of covenant is that of a contract or agreement between two parties. In Scripture, however, covenant has always meant more than this. It signifies a relationship of abiding trust and fidelity with God."[1]

The covenantal relationship, she continues, embodies a "bond of faithfulness," not just with God but with other people. "At the heart of Quaker faith is the understanding that one cannot live God's new order alone. . . . It is necessary to have a community to embody a new pattern of living."[2] In other words, to be faithful to our covenant with God, we are called to be faithful to each other. Likewise, to be faithful in our covenant with each other in our Quaker meetings, we are called to a covenant with God. Friend Tom Gates calls this relationship "members one of another."[3]

The covenant community stands in contrast to the dominant culture construct of a collection of independent individuals who share some similar goals, thoughts, and ideas. This is the biblical idea of one body, many parts (1 Corinthians 12:12–27). Earlier Quakers had a more biblical understanding of covenant community than many Quakers today do. Part of that is because some Quakers struggle with the collective, communal nature of covenant community. Also, even though people may be drawn to Quaker community, there may be resistance to the idea that the community may hold spiritual authority. There are in addition some Friends and some meetings that do not aspire to covenant relationship in their faith communities.

Where there is a sense of covenant community, all members bear at least some of the work of tending to their relationships with each other and with the Divine. Often, particular parts of that tending are laid on the hearts of the elders; it is their spiritual call and leading. Many elders find their hearts drawn to nurture, look after, and care for the community. They give attention to weaving together the spiritual, social, and physical connections of the body as a whole. This work becomes even more vital as climate change and our social-political reality make it more necessary and as it becomes clearer that everything we do has impact beyond our awareness.

It is also true that our current-day Quaker communities look very different than those of early Friends, both spiritually and geographically. Not everyone would consider themselves in a covenantal relationship within their meeting or would even agree with what that might entail. Others are in various places of relationship, something that shifts over time; it is not a static relationship. In addition to people's spiritual relationship to the meeting, there is also a geographic relationship. Some Friends are geographically distant from any monthly meeting—or from a meeting that meets their spiritual condition. There are also many Quaker communities—the wider Quaker fellowship—that Friends may find themselves in. Young adult friends especially long for and seek Quaker community even as they find themselves without geographical roots. Elders with a concern for our sacred community can play a key role in supporting the spiritual lives of these Friends who find themselves in a more nomadic way of life.

Quaker elders do some of their most important work in their monthly meetings, with individuals, and in the many new manifestations of community that are arising among us.

This means that the work will vary. Sometimes it will be more like gardening. Sometimes it will be more like being in the depths of the forest. Sometimes it will be in that liminal space on the edges. Almost always, it will involve transition and an invitation to transformation of some sort.

Reflection on Eldering

The early [Quaker] journals show examples of the relationship of ministers and elders based in listening to the Spirit, elders naming and encouraging ministers, traveling as companions, and holding one another up in joint meetings. Elders were grounded in their meetings, to the extent that if an elder was to move, their status did not generally move with them. Much of the work of the elder was intuitive, related to sensing and naming the work of Spirit within the meeting community. . . .

Without an understanding of "care of the meeting" as the container out of which ministry and spiritual nurture arise, are fostered, and are held accountable to the meeting community, we run the risks of shallowness in our meetings' spiritual life and of lack of accountability.[4]

Lu and Kenn Harper
Rochester Friends Meeting, New York

The work an elder does within the monthly meeting and other Quaker communities is often quite visible—working with individuals or helping to ground a meeting for business, for example. There is another piece, though, that may be invisible to anyone but the elder. It may be found within the mycorrhizae of the community, unseen and unknown by many, yet juicy and fecund, perhaps supporting, praying for, and instigating spiritual openings and growth. Perhaps the work of the elder is hanging out in the energetic auras of the meeting—noticing and working with what is happening in the spaces between and beneath and above and around, in ways unseen and perhaps not understood. These unseen fungi should not be underestimated.

Some eldering is creative and juicy, but some is like doing the dishes or changing diapers; it's less fun. Some of it just excites the elder because it draws us to a higher place. And some of it is much more mundane and less interesting to the elder. But being fun is not one of the criteria. The criteria are what needs to be done and what we are called to.

If we believe that the body of Friends has been gathered by God to do some piece of God's work, then we must tend not just the elements we see—individuals' spiritual lives or communal issues that arise—but also the underlying health of the meeting. In the gardening analogy, this is not just considering the plants; this is considering the health of the dirt of the whole garden, even the total habitat in which the garden grows—the birds, the bees and other insects, and the other plants that are part of the space. In the old-growth forest metaphor, this means being attentive and attuned to the wild places and perhaps accompanying an individual or the meeting as a whole through the wilds. It may also mean an immersion into the mycorrhizae.

All that elders do reflects back to and, it is hoped, builds up the spiritual health of the meeting. Elders hold a vision of a body that is gathered in gospel love, the beloved community. It is believed and hoped that, through the care and work of the elders, the Quaker community is led more deeply and faithfully into God's work. This prayerful attention over time cannot but increase the grounding of the meeting and its experience of God's love.

A helpful metaphor for an elder, as mentioned earlier, is that of the very best kindergarten teacher you could ever imagine. These special people have an innate knack for knowing the best gifts of each of the children in their care. Others of us might describe the individual children as solemn, or overactive, or antisocial, or limited in any one of a hundred ways. These special teachers don't ignore the behavior others of us find troubling, yet they somehow see beyond to the gifts at the core. Then the teacher is able to build just the right environment for these little beings to discover their best self. It may be a building project for one child, a dance experience for the one who can't sit still, a nurturing role for the natural caretaker teamed up with a child who needs to be cocooned, or maybe even building alliances between two kids with similar challenges. This is a great metaphor for elders who, alone or together, are looking after the spiritual gifts in the meeting community.

Reflection on Eldering

As I have served my area meeting as an elder, I have experienced the privilege of being invited to listen to Friends' struggles and leadings, the joys of spiritual awakening as well as their disappointments, frustrations and hurts. Whenever I am invited into someone's life in this way, I am profoundly conscious of the great responsibility and trust involved in the exercise of eldership.[5]

Craig Barnett, Sheffield and Balby Area
Quaker Meeting, England

The Many Facets of Eldering

Many aspects of eldering are needed to support the meeting community. The different colors of the eldering palette are present in varying ways and amounts in our monthly meetings and in the wider Quaker world. Typically, no one elder is gifted in or called to all these different aspects. Some are laser-focused on one area, and others have a broader range of gifts. Gifts of the Holy Spirit come and go, and no individual should be expected to carry the weight of all eldering for the meeting. Elders must be open and nimble enough to yield to the breath of the Spirit, whether in ebb or in flow.

To better understand the actual work of elders, we now turn to some of the 'divine job assignments' that might be given. We do this knowing that the delineations below are, in our experience of the gift of eldering, rarely so clearly defined.

Spiritual Formation of Individuals

Elders' work, at its core, is spiritual formation. One of the taproots of spiritual formation is bringing people closer to God and to that which God longs for them. Thus, elders can have a significant role in individual spiritual nurture, leaning into the belief that we have a responsibility to nurture each other.

There are many ways that spiritual nurture and formation happen, often without those terms being used. Sometimes it may be an established ongoing relationship where two friends get together regularly and often. Sometimes it might be more casual, an on-the-fly or occasional conversation. Sometimes contact will be initiated by the less experienced friend who has an intuitive sense, possibly a leading, that the other individual (who may or may not be overtly recognized as an elder) may be helpful. Or, the work may be initiated by an elder who recognizes that a Friend is at a point in their spiritual development where a bit of attention or nudge might be significant. While each case will be different, elders' efforts and commitment are rooted in their personal experience of the Divine, desire to share that experience, and vision of a body that is gathered by God to do God's work.

One element of how this work nurtures is not just the things that are said but also the consistency of interest and the willingness to be of service on the part of the elder along with the experience of being with a grounded spiritual person on the part of the one being nurtured. The less experienced Friend may not be able to articulate exactly why they want to hang around with the elder but will most often recognize on some level that there is some sense of wisdom, depth, and constancy that is desirable and that rubs off just by being with the elder.

Whether in a structured ongoing relationship or occasionally touching base, the elder will

- encourage the Friend to recognize where the Divine has manifested in their life;

- encourage the Friend to regular reading and retreat;

- discuss the types of prayer and its value in one's life;

- discuss Quaker practice and how all our beliefs and practices derive from an understanding of God in each of us;

- discuss personal theology: "What is your understanding of what God is and how God works in our lives?"

- discuss vocal ministry, issues in the meeting, or issues in the wider world and how one might understand them from a spiritual perspective; and

- encourage the Friend to greater faithfulness, and an understanding of how relatively subtle shifts in their life can begin to manifest in the life of the Spirit.

An elder may also accompany a person through some of the more difficult hurdles of giving up long-held beliefs and understandings that no longer fit them. For example, a particularly challenging aspect of spiritual formation is the notion of submitting—submitting to God and to a body of fallible people who believe they are acting as God would have them act. Another example comes in meetings for business, where it is fine to have an opinion and to voice your view on a subject but then Quakers are encouraged to let go of personal views in favor of the movement of the Spirit. This is so unlike much of our society! The elder can help steer a less experienced Friend through this paradigm shift, helping them to see the joy that lies in submission.

Reflection on Eldering

When I first came to Friends as a twenty-something, I wandered into Berkeley Friends Meeting on Vine Street. I wasn't there but for three meetings for worship when Miriam Berg marched up to me and thrust a copy of *No Cross, No Crown* [a pamphlet written by second-generation Quaker William Penn] into my hand and told me that I must come to the reading and discussion group that met on Wednesday nights. She came with such authority to me and was so clear that that was what I was to do that I didn't even question, and I showed up. At that point, I wasn't a Christian. I'd grown up in a secular humanist home. I hadn't any issue against Christianity, I just hadn't really been exposed to it. But that act, and immersing myself in that book with that small group of people, opened the power of early Friends to me. It was the beginning of a kind of apprenticeship. Apprenticeship requires not just the apprentice but also some master builders, some masters to whom you are apprenticed.

I then became a member of Strawberry Creek Meeting, and I became a member because at my very first experience of [Pacific] Yearly Meeting [Sessions] . . . I ended up in the worship-sharing group with Mary

Shutes, another woman of great weight and authority, who at the conclusion of the yearly meeting worship-sharing sessions called me up and said, "You will return to your meeting and apply for membership." It's like she used Jedi Force, and I just sort of said, "I will return and apply for membership." It was that applying for membership, before I even really knew I was ready or considered myself good enough to be a Quaker—I just knew that I had yoked myself to these people, and I was to become part of this group. . . .

The last story of it [eldering] being enfleshed that I want to share is from Ben Lomond Quaker Center, where I was invited by itinerant traveling minister Bob Schmitt from Northern Yearly Meeting and Elaine Emily from Southern California Quarter of Pacific Yearly Meeting to serve as an elder at a year-end retreat. I had no idea that I had these gifts. They named these gifts and they lifted them up in me and in another person. During the retreat, a group of us had a small meeting for worship much like the traditional Quaker "opportunity" that was so covered and gathered. I have had no experience like it since. But we were yoked to each other, to those traveling ministers, and then through them to our friend Lloyd Lee Wilson . . . who helped to shape and apprentice all of us. The fruits of that gathering and of that group, who stayed together for years with each other, have just blossomed all throughout the Religious Society and beyond.

It all rests, I think, on authority and discipline, the authority that comes through God and the discipline in the monthly meeting. Apprenticeship requires discipline. It requires coming back again and again. It requires a leap of faith into trusting those who are guiding us and also a willingness to learn the tradition. It also requires a clarity of invitation and sometimes generous exclusion.[6]

Kristina Keefe-Perry
Three Rivers Worship Group, Cambridge, Massachusetts

Spiritual Formation of the Community

Through spiritual nurture of individuals, elders also nurture the body—the faith community—in its life in the Spirit. Spiritual formation of the community is deeply rooted work. The elders' role in this includes giving vocal ministry. Some call this an eldering seeding message through which what the elder says opens the way for deep and rich ministry. Elders may also hold vocal ministers in prayer, deepen discernment in meeting for business, encourage participation on committees, be a grounding presence at meeting retreats, and join others in breaking bread together. These all contribute to a meeting's experience of the Divine and to their growth in faith as a community. Just as individuals are called ever closer to God, so are communities. When spiritual formation happens as a communal experience, the release of the Spirit is greater than the sum of the individuals.

One of the important ways Quaker meetings tend to communal spiritual nurture is through the Ministry and Counsel Committee (which sometimes has other names). While not every person on the committee will necessarily be an elder, its members named usually do have some of the gifts and qualities of eldership. And, whatever its make-up, the work of this committee is communal spiritual nurture in its many facets.

The fruit of communal spiritual formation is a worshipping community that is deeply rooted in the Divine and attuned to how Spirit may be nudging and leading the community into greater faithfulness. You may know of faith communities that are acting powerfully in the world, communities that are doing works that are greater than the sum of their numbers. This has been true of Quakers many times in our history.

Care of Worship

Reflection on Eldering

There is no Quaker meeting without the elder, if there's not somebody holding it. If any group of people come together for silent worship, out of that will come the elder and the minister. Where unprogrammed meetings today miss the point is that we're cutting off the flower from our roots. Eldering and ministry are a flower of our meeting for worship. And they come naturally. They will bubble up out of that worship.

Joseph Garren
Middlebury Friends Meeting, Vermont

The meeting for worship is the heart of the Quaker faith. It is where we reach for a collective experience of God's presence. Sometimes this is a peaceful, nurturing experience; other times it may be revelatory, giving us some new understanding of what we are supposed to do or where we have been going astray. Sometimes the experience is wordless, other times it derives from vocal ministry. And, of course, sometimes we are restless and uncentered.

Reflections on Eldering

One of the elders approached me at the rise of meeting to express appreciation for my ministry, and we then talked for several minutes about how important specific feedback is to me and how difficult it is for me to rise to speak during worship. She was surprised, as most Friends seem to be, to learn that speaking in meeting is not the easiest thing in the world for me to do. This Friend was blind and intentionally paid closer attention to sounds, including speech, than anyone else I had encountered. One came away from a conversation with her feeling more deeply listened to and heard than when speaking with nearly any sighted person. It was a gift that was very helpful to her in carrying out the activities of an elder.[7]

Lloyd Lee Wilson
Friendship Friends Meeting,
Greensboro, North Carolina

*****

In the year 1755, being in company with Comfort Hoag and her companion, from New England, then on a religious visit to Friends in this part of the country, I attended a meeting with them, in which I felt a concern to speak to the assembly, but, as usual, evaded it. After meeting Comfort said to me, "David, why didst thou not preach today?" I smiled at the query, seeming to wonder that she should ask such a question, and endeavored to appear innocent and ignorant of any concern of that kind. As she knew nothing of me but what she had felt, (having never before seen or heard of me) she said no more. On the following day a similar concern came upon me, and I evaded it as before. After meeting, Comfort again said to me, "David, why didst thou not preach today?" I endeavored to pass it by as I did before, but she said it was not worth while to evade it, for she was assured that I ought to have preached that day, and that I had almost spoiled her meeting by refraining, which had hindered her service. When I found I could not conceal my faults, I confessed the whole, and told her I had been for more than twenty years in that practice; and then gave her a history of my life from the beginning down to that day. She admired that divine kindness was yet manifested toward me in such manner, seeing I had so long rebelled against it, and then gave me suitable caution and advice.[8]

David Ferris, 1707–1779

Two factors increase the likelihood of the grace of the experience of God's presence. The first is preparation during the week. The more Friends that regularly engage in prayer, spiritual reading, and retirement, the more centered the group can be and the more grist is brought, which on occasion bears fruit in vocal ministry. We also recognize that some Friends, often elders, naturally bring a sense of grounding to the meeting. This is especially true if they intentionally pray for the meeting, both during the week and during the meeting for worship. Many meetings appoint someone to have care of worship. While the outwardly apparent part of the job is to end meeting and preside over announcements, the essence of the role is to help ground the meeting and hold an expectation that the body will receive what it needs, whether through silent grace or divinely inspired vocal ministry. The meeting that lacks enough friends engaging in such support for worship may experience dry, silent worship, "popcorn worship," or too many messages that, even if they are interesting or make good points, are a product more of intellect than of spirit.

Reflections on Eldering

Some very powerful elder work happens in meetings every Sunday morning when, usually it's an older Friend, is just sunk down. And if you just said, "Thank you for holding the meeting or grounding the meeting or eldering," they would say, "What are you talking about?" They're just down there in deep prayer with God. But it is just serving the meeting to an incredible capacity. . . . I think the best eldering of all is that deep prayer of "Let thy will be done by these, thy broken vessels."[9]

Gordon Bishop
Grass Valley Friends Meeting, California

*****

Midwives speak to me, particularly in the context of bringing out messages. Midwives speak to me because the Spirit gets us pregnant. The Spirit inside us gets a life. And if we let it live, it is born. And when it wants to come out as ministry, it's useful to have midwives. It's useful to have a monthly meeting to help give birth to what the Spirit wants to conceive and bring out from it. And here, here I know how important midwives can be in the survival of a child who will become a minister.[10]

Benigno Sanchez-Eppler
Northampton Friends Meeting, Massachusetts

*****

I've been called to nurture the spiritual life of my meeting, both the whole meeting and individuals, for many years now. I rely on guidance to let me know what I can do, so it requires sustained attention and sometimes seeking clearness through a discussion with another Friend or two.

One of the very hardest challenges I have lies in addressing the occasional spoken message in meeting for worship that isn't ministry. It is usually from a Friend, either new or of many years, who doesn't really understand what ministry is, where it comes from, what it feels like, how to test it, and how not to wander with it. Of course, that understanding only comes with spiritual deepening, and it is a related challenge to foster and nurture that. I ask for guidance on how to address it gently and effectively with this Friend, or with the whole meeting. And then I usually get some idea of how to proceed.

I note that a further challenge has come with the Zoom meetings for worship, where we are not gathering in person and thus have no opportunity to speak and listen warmly with a Friend face-to-face. I'm asking for more guidance on this!

Jean Rosenberg
Middlebury Friends Meeting, Vermont

*****

Elders may uphold us from a deep place, one which is sometimes beyond and beneath words, and in that place they may lose connection with what is being said; but they hold our sense of worship. They bring to our meetings a deep connection and grounding. They act as a channel for the Spirit to move, through and within both spoken and silent ministry. Sandra Cronk has said that elders are responsible for keeping avenues of listening spiritually alive. . . .

I heard of a meeting in which ministry was dominated by a few who used meeting for worship as an opportunity for a political rant. Elders, anxious to receive ministry in tender and creative spirit, failed to guide those who ministered, and failed to lead them lovingly to an understanding of what true ministry was. The remaining Friends felt betrayed and disappointed that their spiritual needs had not been met. There was unresolved conflict in the meeting and many left to go to other meetings or left the Society of Friends altogether.[11]

Jenny Routledge
Norfolk & Waveney Area Quaker Meeting, England

*****

It seems worth attempting to shine some light on what we mean by "grounding." With occasional exceptions, the earth we stand on is quite stable. If we stand on the earth in an open spiritual state, we can sense both the limitless energy of stability and its "aliveness," that there is a subtle and deep vibration of the earth, and we can sense the life hidden in the soil: insects and bacteria working. Contrast this with the ephemeral nature of the air above, which can be hot, cold, still, windy, sunny, rainy. And consider the relationship: the sun and the rain provide nourishment for that which grows in the soil, and the earth provides the platform for the rain and the wind—somewhere for the sun to shine.

Being grounded is tapping into that alive stability of the earth, whether you consider it an analogy or see yourself as making a spiritual connection to the earth. Some Friends find it easier than others to tune their bodies and their hearts to that energy, and when they do, that sense of stable groundedness can pervade the room. In practice, the elder may focus for a time on actively reaching for that stable, eternal aspect of the Divine or may simply sink into contemplation or active prayer, both for a sense of God's presence and trusting what is needed will be offered, be it vocal ministry, an internal sense of guidance, or the blessed grace of gathered worship. Thinking in terms of the Trinity, the elder grounding worship is reaching for God the creator and ground of all rather than Christ the teacher.

Some Friends are more easily influenced by the spiritual equivalent of the sun and wind, but the elder is like the string of a kite, providing a connection between the stable earth and the glorious manifestation of sun and wind. Without the string, the kite might be blown away to unknown territory.

Bruce Neumann
Fresh Pond Monthly Meeting
Cambridge, Massachusetts

*****

Morning. Rising. Feeling Fractured.

In anticipation I arrive. . . .

The peace and silence come.

A sense of glowing grace.

I am blessed and I belong.

I am accepted.

I am made whole.[12]

Jan de Voogd, 1932–2021

The Meeting for Business

In Quaker meetings for business, we have the opportunity to practice how the presence of the Divine works through us and how our belief that any one of us may be speaking the Truth informs how we listen and respond. In theory, we are all listening deeply and drop our allegiances and preformed opinions. However, in practice we are flawed humans; we may misunderstand what someone is saying, we may not recognize the log in our own eye, or we may not be able to recognize the difference between a strong personal opinion and a divine leading.

The clerk may be an elder with good listening skills and the ability to sense the message under the words. Whether this is the case or not, there are two significant roles for the elder in meeting for business.

The first role is essential grounding of the meeting. Much like grounding a meeting for worship, this is attempting to be a spiritual channel, ushering the Eternal into the room. By being centered and grounded, the elder can spread a sense of the presence of the Divine, much like a musical tone creates resonance in other objects. Particularly in cases when there is a challenging agenda item, it is useful if a few elders begin to anchor and ground the room and the body in worship before the business meeting begins. It is even better if the meeting names a few to this role. This helps foster the understanding more widely of the importance of grounding and may invite participation in grounding the meeting.

Secondly, as individuals with perhaps a greater understanding of the place of the current moment in the flow of time, and as individuals with the ability to hear the message behind the words, elders may be in a good position to offer a few words to the gathered body that clarify the movement of the Spirit. Or, they may put in perspective the difference between personal interest and the leading of the Spirit. Although the elder's role in gathered bodies is often outwardly silent, there will be moments when their words can help shift the body to a clearer, more Light-filled condition.

Reflections on Eldering

Friends came [to a workshop on eldering at the 2010 annual meeting of the Europe and Middle East Section (EMES) of Friends World Committee for Consultation] with very little experience of what eldership was and many without appointed elders. Several had reported difficulties with maintaining discipline in their business meetings, and the meetings of EMES too struggled at times in this respect. In the first session one of the elders stood up and reminded Friends of the discipline of addressing the table and speaking only once. After that the discipline was held throughout the weekend without any further reminders.[13]

Jenny Routledge
Norfolk & Waveney Area Quaker Meeting, England

*****

In pondering the motion of holding a body of Friends, especially a large body like a yearly meeting, it feels like there is something really important going on that I'm doing or am part of, and yet it also feels like I am so utterly insignificant as to be invisible. The outward visual is simply of a person sitting. I have felt a deep longing to know what is going on in those times. I resonate with naming it as "presence-ing"—a way of being present and holding the space and helping in bringing into the space of the gathered body something that isn't manifest yet, an unimagined possibility.

Janet Gibian Hough
Cobscook Friends Meeting, Whiting, Maine

*****

The recording clerk [in the capacity of elder] simply stays centered, modeling for the body the spirit in which business is best done and holding the clerk, those presenting business, and the body of Friends in love.

Being presiding clerk can be strenuous, challenging the most spiritually robust individual. Having individuals accompanying them who can tell the truth, affirming the positive and offering ideas for reflection, is not necessarily the role of the recording clerk. But before or after the session, the recording clerks may serve as a sounding board and even help a clerk who is struggling with a particular item or individual. Tenderly done, perhaps with some humor, this can support the work of the presiding clerk.

. . . Every role in a meeting calls for the gifts of eldership, of a loving, truthful, courageous, humble care for the spiritual well-being of individuals and the entire meeting.[14]

Karen Reixach
Keene Friends Meeting, New Hampshire

Praying

Many elders are known for their praying capacity. Some are the ones known for having a vital prayer practice. For example, they may keep a list of folks in need of prayer or accompaniment, such as prayers for healing an individual or community or the right holding of a gathering or an emerging ministry. Those in need of prayer know that they want to be on that list. Others who pray are unrecognized by their community or unappreciated. They are often unknown, unacknowledged prayer magnets that hold the spiritual center. When elders with the capacity to hold meeting for worship in deep prayer are present, the verbal and silent

81

worship is palpably, qualitatively different than when the holding is absent (see appendix 4).

Reflections on Eldering

The Society of Friends would soon die out if we could not depend on the silent and inconspicuous prophets who are necessary for each gathered meeting, for if they do not stay faithfully in that living center, how can others 'catch' the spirit which leads us and holds us together? Robert Barclay described this beautifully three centuries ago when he told how the secret, silent, inconspicuous prayer and silent ministry of just one person could lift and center an entire meeting.[15]

William Taber (1927–2005)

*****

The president of Haverford College, back in 1933–1934, . . . was William Wistar Comfort. . . . He sat at the head of the meeting for worship in the old meetinghouse where all the students and faculty sat in worship together at least once a week. I did not hear him say a word in meeting. . . . His silent ministry, radiating love and teachableness, and strength to all of us in the room, is still working good things in me. It is extraordinary to be a former student who can say, "I remember clearly his beautiful silence."[16]

Francis D. Hole (1913–2002)

*****

If someone pays attention to the part of me that struggles to know God, my search intensifies. . . . If someone believes with me in the amazement of grace, prays with me, and reminds me of God's tenderness, I live more thoroughly and bravely in sacred time.[17]

Mary Rose O'Reilley

Discernment

In many meetings, there are members almost everyone wants on their clearness, anchor, and support committees. Individuals seek them out to ask their advice or for a listening ear to help them puzzle through a spiritual dilemma. Some bring the gift of discernment to the clerking table. While all good clerks have some capacity in this area, some are primarily ministers or administrators. Each group will call forth different gifts for a particular time and situation.

It is important to remember that discernment and decision-making are two different motions, though they are connected in that discernment typically leads to a decision. Discernment in the Spirit is more than a list of pros and cons on a particular issue or dilemma. Some elders have a well-tuned antenna for input from the spiritual realm and a sensitivity to how Spirit may be moving us as individuals and as a community. Some may dismiss this as airy-fairy, while some find it perfectly reasonable. Think of gifted, well-schooled musicians. They hear and experience something different and more than those of us who are nearer to tone deaf and unschooled in music. For the latter, the complexities and layers of music are unable to be named or described. In our communities, we often acknowledge and trust the knowing of gifted musicians easier than those gifted in listening to the movement of Spirit.

Elders are those who sense the movement of the Spirit and can name that very early on before it is evident to other people. Elders discern that movement; then they nurture it and cocoon it and call it forward. One metaphor for this is the metaphor of the elder as a midwife. The ministry is not the elder's, but they know something about how to allow the ministry to come forward.[18]

Recognizing and Naming Spiritual Gifts

If we believe, as Paul describes in 1 Corinthians 12 and elsewhere, that each of us has spiritual gifts given to us by God in service of the community, then the meeting has a role in naming and nurturing those gifts. Elders often play a key role in noticing, encouraging, and supporting spiritual gifts in members of the meeting community. This kind of care can be found in nominating committees that are concerned with people's gifts and leadings as well as with the needs of the meeting community.

Reflection on Eldering

When and where the Religious Society of Friends is healthy, the community will recognize, empower, and use gifts in its members. The gift of discerning the presence of gifts in others is a particularly valuable one for a meeting to have. Sometimes, though, a meeting can suppress gifts, as when it collectively disbelieves in the possibility of a gift of eldership, or of healing, or of prophecy.

John Jeremiah Edminster
Clear Creek Meeting, Richmond, Indiana

Elders also work outside the formal committee structure when noticing and naming spiritual gifts. It is sometimes as simple as a quiet comment from one friend to another: "I've noticed the kids seems very engaged when you teach First Day school." Or, "I've really appreciated your insights at the last couple of business meetings." Just noticing and naming can be a powerful support for the individual. Following that up with more conversation, perhaps pointing out the fruits of the Spirit, is encouraging. Eventually, the observant and encouraging elder might make suggestions to the nominating committee. If there is a leading and gift that falls outside the bounds of the monthly meeting structure, the elder might suggest approaching the ministry and counsel committee, where the friend can speak about their concern, the elder can speak to what they have observed, and the committee can discern how the meeting might encourage and support the leading. In some cases, this will result in a committee for support and accountability.

This particular facet of eldering, that of naming gifts, can elicit both pushback and/or dialogue in our unprogrammed meetings. There can be the misunderstanding that noticing, naming, and supporting spiritual gifts means raising some people up above others. Pushback may also come from spiritual jealousy and envy, which stifle spiritual growth individually and communally. There are several things to remember regarding the naming of gifts. We are all different. We all have spiritual gifts. The gifts, while being made manifest within individuals, are for the community. It takes humility and courage to acknowledge your own spiritual gifts as well as the gifts of others.

Some elders have an ability to see connections between people's gifts. Sometimes, this takes the form of networking, of weaving together the spiritual gifts of the community. The elder might say, "Oh, you should talk to that historian." Or, "Marcelle's going to be at my house. Don't you want to come for tea?" This is different from a ministry of hospitality. It is specifically noticing and supporting people's gifts in ministry, even if the ministers do not recognize it as eldering.

Voicing Hard Truths and Rebuking

Speaking hard words to a community or an individual is not something that most elders have a desire to do. Yet Spirit puts this on the to-do list for some. This is some of the most challenging work for an elder. It comes when their eyes are opened to a way the meeting or an individual is falling short of living into the divine life. With that observation, Spirit may then lay it on the elder's heart to speak the hard truth of what they see, with the hope of creating a nudge toward greater faithfulness.

The work of voicing hard truths is made even more difficult when it involves rebuking, to use a traditional Quaker term. By rebuke, we mean speaking to a condition or action that needs repentance. It is a call for an individual or meeting to change their ways, to change their behavior, to return to good order. In one yearly meeting, a person rebuked the body for laying down its children's committee, saying that it was not rightly ordered. A classic example in Quaker literature is the story of Samuel Bownas being rebuked: "Thou comest to meeting as thou went from it (the last time), and goes from it as thou came to it, but art no better for thy coming."[19] An example of a hard truth that is not a rebuke might be a message to a retreat leader that their cognitive ability is diminished and they may need to lay down their ministry.

Reflection on Eldering

Oh! the necessity of labouring for good order! and Oh that it may be done with tenderness, meekness, love, and forbearance! For I do not believe that labours bestowed more in order to cut off, than to reform and restore, will ever reach the true witness in the minds of offenders. But when offenders are laboured with in the spirit of meekness and love, with an earnest desire for their amendment, welfare, and restoration, (the only right way and object of labouring with them), it is pretty certain, if their day is not over, to reach the witness, more or less, in their mind, and to fix such an evidence therein, that though they may reject and spurn at such faithful labours, and those who thus bestow them; yet, if ever such offenders feel the tendering visitations of divine grace, powerfully extended to them, they can, and generally will, look back upon the labours bestowed on them by their brethren, and have a feeling testimony and acknowledgment in their minds, that they have been sought unto and laboured with in love, good-will, and tenderness.[20]

Job Scott, 1751–1793

Friends today may balk at the word "rebuke" and the notion of speaking hard truths that point out a fault in another Friend or within a community. It is good to bring some caution to this eldering task because the elder needs to avoid several very harmful pitfalls. One pitfall comes if the elder rebukes someone as a way to try to impose control on a person or situation. The speaking of words of rebuke or hard truths may also come from a place of arrogance or self-righteousness, which may blind the elder to their own errors and distortions. Another pitfall comes when a misguided attempt at eldering upholds Quaker cultural norms that are harmful to the community.

We want to be clear that by rebuke we do not mean policing the meeting or keeping order. Historically, rebukes happened when a Friend was seen to be walking in a disorderly way. Also historically, rebukes have been abused and have done harm. Both motions—the helpful and the harmful rebukes—remain true in our times. It is important to remember that rebukes should not come from a person's rigid, ungrounded sense of what is right or wrong. They should not be used to attempt to keep Spirit from breaking through. Many of our stories of poor and hurtful eldering come from people abusing rebukes. It is almost always inappropriate for an elder to rebuke someone the elder does not know. Likewise, after giving a rebuke, the elder is almost always required to accompany the person, at least for a little while. The rebuke, when used rightly, is intended to bring the Friend back into right order and stronger into community.

Reflections on Eldering

When . . . we [as elders] encounter sin, we can meet it with even greater portions of love, allowing God's power to work where we in our human limitations cannot.[21]

Susan Smith
Rockingham Monthly Meeting, Harrisonburg, Virginia

*****

An ex-clergyman spoke in meeting for the first time. When he heard ministry from a Friend who in his opinion was wrong in his interpretation of the Bible, he rose and spoke to put the meeting right. Afterwards a Friend spoke to him lovingly and directly, telling him this was not the way of Friends. The elder's approach was kind and welcoming, and he invited him to visit his home. The new attender was not offended but felt heard and acknowledged. The elder died recently and at his memorial meeting the new attender, now a weighty Friend, spoke movingly of the significance of this 'eldering'.

Another meeting was very disturbed by an elderly Friend who took notes during ministry and then read them aloud to the meeting. For some time the meeting took no action. Eventually an elder stood silently with him until he stopped speaking and resumed his seat. When she spoke to him afterwards, she asked lovingly why he made notes and read them aloud. He replied that this was his way of dealing with his failing memory. She told him that his presence in meeting was greatly valued by Friends. He ceased the practice and he seemed to find a peace. It appeared that his behaviour had in part also been an attempt to contribute to and be acknowledged by his own meeting.[22]

Jenny Routledge,
Norfolk & Waveney Area Meeting, England

It is illuminating to note that earlier Quakers lived in covenant community and better understood and accepted the authority of the meeting as being of divine origin than many Friends today, who are influenced by our culture's independent-minded idolization of the individual and by stories of poorly conceived eldering. Friends are often uncomfortable with the idea that an individual, Spirit-led and grounded in a meeting community, might have the authority to speak such truths. This reinforces the need for such difficult motions of eldering to be grounded in love.

Reflections on Eldering

I had attended a meeting in New Jersey for two years as a sojourner after moving from the District of Columbia, where I had held membership for thirty-three years. A member of the meeting's committee with responsibility for membership matters requested a visit with me. She wanted to discuss my intention regarding membership in my new meeting and, in doing so, she carried the eldering function. After she greeted me warmly and we caught up with each other's lives, she asked some searching questions. First, she patiently listened and learned of the challenges involved in changing my membership. We reached a mutual understanding concerning my situation. She accepted and understood.

After that, she shared the concern that I should move my membership as soon as I was spiritually and practically ready. She talked of the benefits to the meeting of my committing to be a part of the corporate body. We then went on to reach clarity about the next steps. I volunteered that, God willing, I would change my membership in a year or less. . . . Wanting to be accountable, I encouraged her to stay in touch about the matter. After a time of prayer, she left.[23]

Margery Mears Larrabee, 1919–2008

*****

Quakers need to get MUCH clearer about our collective boundaries. I have often joked that it might take someone practicing animal sacrifice in the middle of the

Meetinghouse floor before we would rise up and say no. Even then, some Friends would be looking around to see that someone else besides themselves would speak. It would help if individual committees got clear about behaviors that are and are not acceptable within their area of attention. (Could the property committee be clear that we do not allow practices that damage the building? Could worship and ministry be clear that we do not allow other forms of worship to occur during our worship? Would either of those boundary clarifications empower someone to say no to the animal sacrifice example?) This is where we need to return to our eldering practices—if we could speak early and lovingly to those who we feel are engaging [in] behavior that is disruptive to the community we could resolve many things. This is your sacred community—if you won't speak for it then how will it remain sacred?[24]

Lynn Fitz-Hugh
Olympia Friends Meeting, Washington

*****

This is a place [Numbers 14:11–19], one of the very first places in the Bible, where God gets eldered. God gets eldered by his minister [Moses]. And it is a lesson to all of us. And the Spirit speaks to me, saying, "What kind of relationship do you have with the Spirit that makes you minister? What kind of relationship do you have with the God that loves you into the work? Can you talk back to the Spirit that moves you?"

Here, Moses is absolutely dead on, reminding God of how God himself defined himself very early on in their relationship. . . . This is a huge, cheeky thing that Moses does because God is upset and God is saying, "Let's clear them out!' And Moses says, "Um, you know, that's not going to look very good." . . .

Moses is saying here, "You know, you told me that you were merciful, all-forgiving, etc., etc., and why don't you try going back to that?" And God knew that Moses was right.[25]

Benigno Sanchez-Eppler
Northampton Friends Meeting, Massachusetts

*****

One of the most important aspects of eldering is avoiding judgment. We need to separate the person from the behavior. This can be difficult, especially when the behavior is upsetting to me personally or shows up a weakness in me. One thing I have learned over the years is that human beings have social, spiritual, emotional, and other needs that are as essential to our survival and well-being as physical needs. When those needs are not being met, we behave inappropriately. If I can discern what needs are not being met, it is easier to deal with the behavior rather than judging the person. It certainly doesn't excuse the behavior but perhaps can make it more understandable.

Deborah Wood
Purchase Quaker Meeting, West Harrison, New York

Some of the hard truths that an elder might be spiritually called to name for the benefit of the meeting are fundamental to the foundation of the community—that the meeting is in a difficult spot, for example, or that the body is not spiritually grounded. Other issues revolve around individuals and their impact on the meeting:

- Mental illness. Most of us carry some "baggage" from an earlier part of our lives, and it affects how we see and interact with the world. For some, the baggage is relatively minimal; others have learned to minimize the effects on their behavior and their lives and others; some are unaware of their effect on people. In addition, there are serious mental health issues such as personality disorders. These don't necessarily need meeting intervention, though they may when they are untreated.

- Prophet or visionary. Although our faith tradition was founded on a new vision of how to live a Christian life, we can be very uncomfortable with continuing revelation and the emergence of new understandings of what we are called to. Our own history is littered with Friends we celebrate now who were not well received in their own meetings. John Woolman and Benjamin Lay are two examples. There are prophets among us now whom many find hard to stomach.

- The Confounder or Adversary. Many Quakers have experienced a meeting for business, a meeting for worship, a conflict in the meeting, or any number of other situations, including within themselves, where something uncomfortable and nameless emerges. It is a 'something' that may even feel spiritually dangerous. In fact, it may actually *be* spiritually dangerous. When this happens in a meeting for business, it "confounds" the possibility of unity. When it happens in a meeting for worship, the worship may feel jangly and unsettled. Occasionally, this energy can be seen to be centered in an individual. This energy may happen even when those involved are spiritually mature and prepared. It is an energy that appears, unbidden, and works against our sense of God's loving presence. Some Friends prefer not to talk about the Adversary because they believe that kind of attention gives it power. Others think it is not real. Others do not want to know about it. We believe it can be important to name this energy because, by naming it, we have a more accurate framework for addressing it. Anything we ignore has the chance to grow and gain power.

- Challenge to our equilibrium. God may at some point feel that our body of people is too complacent and will find someone to stir up our simple good feeling. This is usually not a welcome event, even though it is something the meeting needs for growth and it often leads to a good end.

- Human need for a scapegoat. While our faith teaches us to model our behaviors after the Teacher, our humanness emerges sometimes, and it may be convenient to project our more base thoughts and feelings onto someone else. This is not typically a conscious action. Nonetheless, when this happens, it is as hurtful and destructive as it is when it is intentional, and sometimes more so.

The elder's role in these situations ranges from helping the meeting to see how this uncomfortable situation may be a useful challenge to a deeper understanding of our faith to helping the meeting understand and heal from wounds. It is also important to note that doing nothing often enables destructive behavior. Elders can help a meeting face this truth.

One way elders do their work in this arena is by helping Friends to see the sometimes complicated relationship between the challenges an individual may present and the gifts they bring. It is too easy or facile to observe some egregious behavior and name the individual as a "problem." But we are complicated beings, and we bring all our complexities wherever we show up. The seasoned elder is well suited to deep observation, sympathy, and the willingness to engage where others may retreat.

In this work, the elder must balance concern for both the spiritual health of individuals and the health of the meeting. There are occasions when an individual's mental health issues are extreme enough that they are not only beyond the ability of people in the meeting to understand and deal with but they are detrimental to the well-being of the meeting. In these extreme cases, the individual may be asked to leave the meeting. This is not a decision to take lightly or to be made by any one person, but the elder may have a key voice in the discernment.

The tension between tending to a person with mental health issues and the larger group became apparent at a retreat at Powell House in New York State. A new attender at a small Quaker worship group, whom we will call Alice here, was interested in attending a Powell House retreat. The retreat leader invited her to ride with her to the retreat. As they were driving to the retreat, Alice said things that became increasingly bizarre. When they stopped for gas, the retreat leader made a quick, panicked call to the woman who was serving as elder for the retreat. Once they reached Powell House, the retreat leader told the director what was happening. The retreat began uneventfully. But sometime during that first night, Alice created major chaos, taking out each plate in the kitchen and putting salt on it, for example, and deconstructing a 3-D puzzle and distributing the puzzle pieces throughout the building and the grounds.

The elder came to the retreat leader's room very early in the morning and told her what had happened. It was clear that Alice needed medical assistance, so the sheriff was called to take her to the hospital. At Powell House, a small group of people—all gifted elders, who were there as participants—gathered to put things to rights and to pray and discern with the retreat leader how to go forward with the retreat. The participants were told what had happened, and the group together prayed for Alice. Miraculously, the retreat continued deeply and beautifully. Spirit moved among the group that weekend, facilitated by the elders who gave so generously of their time and gifts.

Reflections on Eldering

Sometimes, when grounding and holding large gatherings of Quakers during Meeting for Worship for Business when Friends were considering important and divisive matters, without understanding why, I would begin attacking myself internally. I came to understand this as a response to an energy or spirit that some might call chaos or the Adversary, something apart from the people in the room. On such occasions, I learned to ground myself deep in my core being by turning or bringing my awareness to a protective presence, an expansive Love, the Divine Mother, the Inward Light. Light brings us love, and there is love also in the fertile darkness of the earth—a darkness which is good. The darkness of the Adversary is dangerous, and there is Light that can pierce and destroy. And, sometimes what seems like the Adversary is something we need to move towards, wrestle with, and move through. This is how I understand discernment of the spirits in the room, in the body, and at work in me.

Janet Gibian Hough
Cobscook Friends Meeting, Whiting, Maine

At one meeting that I was part of, there was a person who was quite paranoid. When he spoke during worship, his ramblings were very hurtful to many. The clerk defended him, saying that there were messages for some people in what he said. Finally, he said something that was hurtful to her. Then the clerk stopped defending him. The meeting requested help from the quarterly meeting and did a lot of seasoning to try to resolve the issue. Eventually, after much work, the meeting united to take action to bar him from attending meeting for worship with a restraining order.

Anonymous

*****

There was a powerful young rising minister who was drinking too much and had inappropriate connections with women. As an elder, I spoke with this person, telling him, "People are asking me about the possibility of you being a keynote speaker at a Quaker event, and I have to say no because your drinking is inappropriate, your sexual behavior is devastating to women, and you have got to stop." His response was, "Don't ever recommend me unless I'm in good order." And he did the work to get his life in good order. This is the only rebuke I have ever given.

Anonymous

*****

Rebukes do not always result in introspection and change of behavior. In one meeting, there was an individual who had what several elders felt was an over-inflated sense of his own spirituality, believing that everything he said was right and true and that what other people in the meeting said was always suspect. Two Friends from the meeting met with him and spoke about what they observed and how his behavior did not fit with their sense of Quaker practice, that Truth is to be found not in the words of one individual but in the discernment of the body. The Friend did not accept the rebuke and did not alter his ways. This person eventually left the Quaker community.

Anonymous

*****

A new attender brought with her to worship a recording of a song. She played the song during worship. In a misguided effort at eldering—called "rogue eldering" by some—several friends rebuked her after worship and ruptured the budding relationship she had with the meeting. A skilled elder could have handled it differently. Rather than rebuking the person, the elder could have asked questions and helped the woman understand why what she did would not typically be appropriate.

Anonymous

*****

A traveling minister was not in good order vis-à-vis the work she was doing in ministry. Her support committee worked with her, but nothing changed. The support committee brought their concern to the Ministry and Worship Committee where the travel minute was held. In that committee, there was a moment of noticing two very important truths. First, the committee noticed the minister's very real gifts of ministry. Second, the committee needed to tell her that she had been out of good order. For at least one of the people involved, this felt very much like a rebuke.

Anonymous

*****

Today, individual Friends are seldom disciplined for any infraction of what former Friends would have called 'right order'—that is, conduct in keeping with religious teachings. Instead of discipline, we trust in counseling and conflict resolution with its emphasis on mediation. We hope for a 'win-win situation' where everyone is happy. . . . While this can be effective if the offending party is open to counsel, it can involve many lengthy sessions that often prove fruitless since there are no consequences to ignoring the counsel.

I have been involved with Quakers for many years at the local, yearly meeting, and national level. It has been my experience that we can do a better job of dealing with conflict if we recover our tradition of discipline by appropriate bodies within monthly, quarterly, and yearly meetings. I've seen the positive fruit of recovering a comprehensive eldering tradition of both nurture and discipline in my monthly and yearly meeting.

It has been our experience that Quaker communities that fail to exert discipline in an open way through properly recognized channels will slip into unofficial discipline through tale-bearing, back-biting, and shunning of offending individuals. When meetings fail to openly discipline through approved channels, a passive-aggressive approach to discipline is all too common among us.[26]

Herb Lape
Westbury Quaker Meeting, New York

Any elder can find themselves needing to give voice to hard truths and rebukes. Some elders are called often to this work. It is important to remember that even if an elder gains some experience in this work and is good at it, it doesn't necessarily mean that it is only that one person's job. This is part of what the community is called to, and elders help support that.

For elders who are called to this work, it is important that they regularly examine their motives. This is best done with other elders rather than alone. It is imperative that, as much as possible, the truth someone speaks comes from love, untainted and mature, without the taste of anger and past hurts. It is much harder to recognize and receive hard truths when they are mixed with the truth-teller's baggage. Given that we are all human, this is sometimes how hard truths come to us—mixed in with everyone's baggage.

This is challenging work. We must emphasize that it requires the elder to be deeply grounded and spiritually convicted in order to be able to speak with the authority of the Divine and to be prepared for pushback. It may take time to accept hard truths because the receiver of the message may experience some anger or other form of resistance or stubbornness.

Remember that part of the elder's job assignment is to do the work of maturing spiritually. This provides the foundation for the elder to be faithful and prepared with a freedom from encumbrances so that they can be a vessel of the Spirit and give the right words to hard truths and rebukes.

Whether speaking hard truths or rebuking, it is vital that the elder do the following:

- discern well how to approach a person and what to say, ideally discerning with others rather than alone, which may take a longer period of time than some would prefer;

- come from a place of humility, with a heart of love and a spirit grounded in God;

- seek the Spirit and the other's greater faithfulness rather than seek to control or bring into conformity;

- recognize that the hard truths or rebukes are an aspect of spiritual formation; and

- pray for the greater good of the person who is not in right order with the intent and hope of strengthening community bonds while releasing any illusion of or effort at control of the process, the person, or Spirit.

Those who are called to this aspect of eldering have the burden and gift of being given a message to deliver to the community or individual. The fact about hard truths is that they are hard to speak and hard to hear, regardless of how faithful one is being. Done well, truth-tellers neither avoid conflict nor add to the disruption. Done well, there will be a new opening for a course correction that brings people back into right order and into deeper community.

In the introduction to the republication of Samuel Bownas's book of advice to Quaker ministers and elders, William P. Taber Jr. summarizes Bownas's life, drawing from his journal, *An Account of the Life, Travels, and Christian Experiences in the Work of the Ministry of Samuel Bownas* (1756). Taber recounts:

Samuel records in his journal that at a First Day meeting in late 1696:

> . . . a young woman, named Anne Wilson, was there and preached; she was very zealous, and fixing my eye upon her, she with a great zeal pointed her finger at me, uttering these words with much power: "A traditional Quaker, thou comest to meeting as thou went from it (the last time) and goes from it as thou came to it, but art no better for thy coming; what wilt thou do in the end?" This was so pat to my then condition, that, like Saul, I was smitten to the ground, as it might be said, but turning my thoughts inward, in secret I cried, "Lord, what shall I do to help it?" and a voice as it were spoke in my heart saying, "Look unto me, and I will help thee;" and I found much comfort, that made me shed abundance of tears.

After this meeting the change in [Samuel Bownas's] life was remarkable:

> I longed for the meeting-day, and thought it a very long week. When the time of meeting came, my mind was soon fixed and staid upon God, and I found an uncommon enjoyment that gave me great satisfaction, my understanding being opened, and all the faculties of my mind so quick, that I seemed another man.[27]

Bownas no doubt felt some strong emotions, perhaps even resistance, when he was told he was coming to meeting for worship and leaving unchanged, but Wilson's message turned his life around.

Listening Ministry

Elders are often known for their particular gift of deep listening, which is something more than simply not speaking. Listening beyond the words and below the words is one of the foundational spiritual gifts of elders. Deep listening creates a sacred space into which a soul can speak and into which a soul can hear more clearly. Deep listening creates space for deep and prophetic speaking.

> What I'm trying to construct here is a theory of attention that depends little on therapeutic skills and formal training: listening like a cow. Those of you who

grew up in the country know that cows are good listeners. And barns, as I said before, are great contemplative spaces—at least the old ones were. I recommend to you this kind of dairy barn listening. We don't need fixing, most of us, as much as we need a warm space and a good cow. Cows cock their big brown eyes at you and twitch their ears when you talk. This is a great antidote to the critical listening that goes on in academia, where we listen for the mistake, the flaw in the argument. Cows, by contrast, manage at least the appearance of deep, openhearted attention.

If you are listening, if you are turning your big brown or blue eyes on somebody and twitching your ears at them, you are earning your silage. You are listening people into existence. You are saving lives. You are producing Grade A.[28]

Mary Rose O'Reilley

Elders know that when they turn their eyes on the people in their community and twitch their ears at them, they are also giving that same openhearted listening attention to the Divine. They are tuning in to the wavelength of the Spirit. There are elders who embody this charism, and in that sacred listening they may then become a channel for the divine energy, presence, and love as it pours out into the community.

History and Good Order

Some elders are steeped in Quaker history and tradition. With their knowledge, they are a rich resource regarding a meeting's desire for and efforts toward living in good order. By good order, we mean a life aligned with God's kin-dom here on earth, a life in tune with Jesus' teachings, a life rooted in the greatest good.

Our understanding of history and good order is subject to continuing revelation, just like the rest of our understanding of the Divine. Elders who know our history and our traditions of good order keep us aware of the vibrancy of and spiritual connection to our Quaker foremothers and forefathers. They help us understand our spiritual traditions, including the reasons and the spiritual convictions around those practices, rather than just rigidly enforcing dogma regarding how things must be done.

This includes guidance on how to keep our practices and understanding from becoming more secularized. Secularization isn't necessarily continuing revelation. In fact, it may be the total opposite. This also may include invitations into discernment about when a tradition is a flower to keep and tend and when it is something that no longer has a good use or perhaps never did.

While our traditions and history are important to inform our way forward, it is equally important to not allow our history to dictate and confine our way forward.

Care and Accountability

Elders are often the ones who, with much love and tenderness, call for accountability in the group and individuals. They expect us to be our best selves and are not afraid to remind us of that to which we aspire. Sometimes, this call to accountability comes in one-on-one relationships, and sometimes it comes in meeting for worship and meeting for business. Accountability here means holding one another to faithfulness to God's call and claim on our life.

Care and accountability may occur informally, one-on-one. It is also increasingly common for individuals to have a care and accountability committee that comes under the care of the meeting; these are sometimes called an anchor or support committee. In these committees, the members serve as elders for the minister and the ministry, whether the call into ministry is time-limited or ongoing and sustained. A care and accountability committee may begin as a clearness committee as the person discerns the call. It is good when a care and accountability committee is grounded in the individual's home meeting. Sometimes, though, this is not ideal or possible. Whatever the make-up of the committee, it is a place where the individual is held in love and care with attention to a faithful response to the leading.

It can be a challenge for a Friend to submit to the authority of the meeting in the form of an accountability committee and to the authority of the Spirit as the One who has laid the leading on the individual's heart. At the same time, the minister and the committee members often find that they are pulled into a greater depth of faithfulness than they imagined possible.

Committee members hold the minister accountable to the continuing unfolding of the ministry. They may also discern with the Friend the next evolutions of the ministry and leading, which may include laying the ministry down. As the intermediary between the minister and the larger meeting, the committee is also charged with helping the meeting stay informed and engaged in the work that has arisen from within their gathered body. If the elders of the committee feel that the calling is true but the meeting is challenged by it, the elders have a role in helping the meeting through their hesitancy to a celebration of the Divine working in their midst.

The yoke is sometimes used as a metaphor for how we engage with our work, the yoke being the device historically used to transmit the power of the beast of burden to the plow. If we imagine that a leading is a weight placed on our shoulders with the expectation of moving forward, then the fit of that yoke is critical to our being able to sustain our efforts. The care and accountability committee is charged with carefully "fitting" the yoke to the individual. This may take the form of cautioning the minister against taking on too much too quickly or moving too fast or too slow, or helping them find the spiritual resources to nourish their work. In other cases, the committee may suggest to the minister that the yoke is fit well and that the field needs plowing and they should lean into the work.[29]

Reflection on Eldering

Yokemates is a term that has emerged for us in naming the experience of working together in service to the Spirit to liberate the message. We were co-leading the workshop; in this case Elaine was serving in the minister function, and I was in the elder function. It has been our experience, in spiritually accompanying over one hundred Friends between the two of us, that eldering provides fuller, richer, truer liberation of the message for the community's benefit.[30]

Cathy Walling
Chena Ridge Friends Meeting, Fairbanks, Alaska

Presence

Some elders hold and exude a strong sense of presence, sometimes called a ministry of presence. This is a presence without an agenda. One way to describe this is that elders with this gift have a spaciousness to which people are drawn. It is, in a sense, a ministry of hospitality in that people are invited into that spaciousness unequivocally, without judgment. This presence is often just being a very steady, maybe silent witness to whatever is happening, whether birth, death, conflict, or a deep spiritual opening. It may also be a place where rest and healing may occur. Often, people gravitate to elders who have this gift of presence.

Reflections on Eldering

The ministry of presence is where all other ministry begins. Presence is a state of being, not doing. Such states are not highly valued in our culture. We prefer action. So those who watch others rise to speak in meeting or travel under the weight of a concern might not recognize their own calling to the ministry of true presence—the ministry of simply 'being with' another person or group.

True presence has a quality of quiet 'every-dayness' to it. Think about a down comforter bringing a sense of coziness and security on a cold, dark night. Or a radiator filling a room with warmth from a source elsewhere. Or some friends sharing cool drinks on a shady porch on a summer's day, talking about nothing in particular, if they're talking at all.[31]

Ann Davidson and Carol Holmes Alpern
Gwynedd Friends Meeting, Gwynedd, Pennsylvania,
and Scarsdale Friends Meeting, Scarsdale, New York

*****

This patient has coded twice and his family are out in the hallway, crying. They ask me to pray over the patient (though not with them—it's complicated). When I see the doctors and nurses are starting to clean up, I ask if I can come in and pray over the patient. I pray for him, for God to hear the prayers of his heart, and for the family and the medical team to care for him with love, compassion, steady hands, and the wisdom to know how best to help him. I pray, knowing that my prayer is being witnessed by the medical team. This space is sacred, and they are a sacred part of it. . . .

The thing about holding space is that once I started, it became a habit. . . . If I believe that God is present in each person, and that God is present in each situation, then I am empowered to name it, to demonstrate the belief, to remind people that their lives and the spaces they occupy can be sacred. . . . In this way, eldering a meeting for business is not dissimilar from showing doctors and nurses that they are included in my prayer. . . . I hold space. I hold it in the same ways at work and in the meetings. I trust that Spirit/God/Christ moves in us and I remind people by my presence, which is grounded in the Presence.[32]

Beth Kelly
Brooklyn Monthly Meeting, New York

*****

I find myself engaged in welcoming the formerly incarcerated home, especially those that attended [Quaker] worship services while inside. Trying to keep them connected to Friends and meetings is something I would like for them because it has enriched my life. I see Quakers as family. Former prisoners need good families to teach that which they have never known: an appreciation of life and the people in it.[33]

Angel Ramos
Rochester Friends Meeting, New York

Of course, not all elders perform all of the functions mentioned in this chapter, and a meeting is blessed if it has elders among them who manifest many or most of these gifts. It is also clear from this discussion of how elders care for meetings that the common perception that eldering is correction is very much incomplete. The elders among us respond in many ways to the call to the ministry of eldership, whether that ministry is in the garden, the wilderness, or the liminal space in between.

Queries for Reflection and Discussion

- What do you see as the work of the elder?

- During a period when others are caught in controversy or spiritual challenges, how can elders help ground the meeting with the belief in the essential rightness that the body has gathered and that the tempest will subside?

- The work of elders often happens in the quiet places, in holding a vision and in praying for the body. Do you give yourself enough time in those quiet places for the work to take place within you?

Interlude 6

Community Disruptions and Elders

Bruce Neumann
Fresh Pond Monthly Meeting, Cambridge,
Massachusetts

From time to time in the life of most meetings, situations arise that disrupt the sense of unity in and with the Spirit and community. This might be an unsettling message in meeting for worship, a passing comment during social hour, or one individual standing in opposition to the sense of the meeting when considering business. It might be a bully in meeting or an abusive relationship.

In any of these situations, the elder can play a significant role in working to restore trust and unity. While the value of a spiritually grounded presence in the midst of an emotional or conflictual time cannot be underestimated, the elder may have a more specific role, engaging in patient and tender exploration with all parties and offering leadership in how to move forward and a vision that conflict is not a failure but an opportunity for deeper relationship. An understanding of both the practice and the conceptual undergirding of gospel order is of great benefit.

Gospel order as a *concept* suggests that God longs for all Creation to be in right relationship. You might consider this as a return to the garden of Eden or the realization of the kin-dom of heaven on earth. All our practices of waiting, listening, and discernment are grounded in the belief that we are working, however slowly, toward that manifestation.

The *practice* of gospel order refers to the ways we interact with each other that are founded on our belief, based on our tradition, that how we approach unity in the Spirit is as important as our belief that unity is possible. The way we approach each other must be in accord with Jesus' teaching to love each other. We may be required to take the plank out of our own eye as part of the process. Our tendency, whether innately human or a product of the wider society, is to polarize into "right vs. wrong," where most often we are "right" and the other is "wrong." Gospel order eschews this notion, suggesting instead that the most important concern is for us to deepen in our relationship with each other and with the Divine—for us to be open to spiritual transformation.

We all know how it feels to be told that something we did is wrong, and our usual, very human reaction is to be defensive. How different a model it is to say: "What you said does not agree with my sense of what God wants for us, and it has put a rift in our relationship, which I would like to restore. Can we talk so I can better understand your point of view?" The Friend who may have made a poorly conceived comment will experience the most growth in understanding if the conversation is engaged with love and tenderness.

The elder may go into this conversation gently holding to their view on the matter, yet they must have an openness to change. This is much like the correct posture for meeting for business. It is fine to go into the meeting with a preliminary opinion, but we must go with hearts and minds prepared, meaning we have studied the materials available and prayed on the topic at hand. We also must have our hearts and minds ready to be moved by the Spirit to an unexpected understanding of how we are led forward.

The resolution of an issue may take five minutes or several meetings or longer. It may take the form of a simple acknowledgment of understanding or an apology to an individual or the meeting. It may also take some work on the elder's part to help others understand the basis of the comment or position. In most cases, there will be a sense of rightness and a deeper understanding of each other and the ways God works with and through us.

Interlude 7

Listening to the Needs of the Meeting and Responding to Nudges from God

Krista Barnard

San Francisco Friends Meeting, California

Space had opened up. My term as co-clerk of Ministry and Oversight Committee had ended a month earlier, and, to my surprise, the Nominating Committee had asked me to serve as co-clerk of Welcoming Committee. My new role included organizing the schedule of greeters in the meetinghouse lobby and doing the greeting myself once every couple of months. The burden was light. Space had opened up, and an image that had been in my mind for many years became stronger, more insistent.

After meeting for worship ends, people drink coffee and tea, eat snacks, and stand or sit while chatting. My image was of a particular table where people could intentionally gather if they wished to focus on deeper topics, such as how is God moving in our lives? I could host such a table myself. I was in Bible study that day, June 4, 2017, with a group of people with whom I had been reading and discussing the Bible for many years. I asked what they thought, and they encouraged me. That night, I wrote to the new co-clerks of Ministry and Oversight proposing my idea to start the following Sunday.

With Ministry and Oversight's permission, I set up such a table labeled with a sign (Join the conversation!) and wrote an announcement to be read at the rise of meeting for worship. The first gathering at the spiritual conversation table went well, with one child, two adult regulars, and one visitor from another country joining me to discuss topics such as What happened in meeting for worship? In a notice to the meeting's Google group, I reported what had happened and said that I would continue the experiment for three more Sundays. The announcement to be read at the rise of meeting included other questions: How do I know when to speak in worship? How do you deepen your spiritual life between meetings for worship? I continued after those three weeks, and I continue to host these gatherings almost three years later.

The same month that I started the table, I also adopted responsibility for the wall of nametags in the lobby. Many nametags belonged to people who had not attended in years, and many regular participants had no nametag. Part of welcoming people into the community and recognizing their regular participation is making them permanent nametags so that they don't have to continue to write their names on new self-stick labels each week. I asked people to give me their name if they wanted me to make them a printed nametag in a badge holder. I created a computer template somewhat similar to the appearance of older nametags that had been made by a calligrapher and began making new nametags.

As I listened to the needs of the meeting and nudges from God, my tasks began to braid together, and I changed what I was doing. My written announcement included the sentence "Newcomers and visitors are particularly welcome," but those words read aloud mean much less than a personal invitation, so I would try to walk over to at least one newcomer at the rise of meeting to ask them to join me at the table. I let them know that any questions about Quakerism were welcome, not just the announced topics. I later began offering to add the newcomers, if they wished, to the meeting's monthly newsletter subscription list and to the Google group. If I noticed someone had been attending for some time, I also offered to make a nametag for them. How is my relationship with God changing my life? My shyness, my tendency to speak only to those whom I already know, is giving way to the work I am called to do in the community.

Despite suggestions to move the discussion to a quieter room than the social hall, I did not do so except on those Sundays when singing at the piano near the table occurred. I felt that the barrier to entry must be as low as possible and that a newcomer, or a tentative person, or a person with only 10 minutes before they had to leave would be less likely to join us if they had to go down the hall to the office or through the door into the kitchen. Sometimes, in the midst of the hubbub, we fell into two conversations, one at each end of the table, because we could not hear each other clearly across the length of the table. That was fine.

I began to write a new announcement each week, inviting us to reflect together on different topics. I realized that the audience for the questions included all those who heard the announcement after worship, not just those who came to the table. In the fall, my participation in three Quaker Center programs, two in Ben Lomond and one brought to San Francisco Friends Meeting by Bob and Kathy Runyan of Ben Lomond Quaker Center, fertilized my growing understanding of ways to support the spiritual life of the meeting. Beginning in October, I expanded the announcement to an email version to our entire Google group, many of whom do not come regularly to meeting for worship or are out of the room attending to children or refreshments when the announcements are read aloud. On Wednesday evenings, after our midweek meetings for worship, I began hosting a discussion seeded by watching a QuakerSpeak video together. Midweek worship needed more care than we had been giving it; it is small, often entirely silent, and includes some participants who do not come on Sundays.

At the video viewings, I was surprised at how strong the interest was in Quaker history. This response helped me come to understand the scope of my call: beyond creating spaces to encourage spiritual conversation, I must also be prepared to provide some education and to promote connections with other Quaker bodies. I began to include links in the emailed announcements for Sunday and Wednesday discussions—links to Bible passages; to sections of various books of faith and practice; to historical and contemporary Quaker and other writings, including our periodicals; and to videos. I began to carry Pink Dandelion's *The Quakers: A Very Short Introduction* in my backpack so that I would at least have that source handy when seeking answers to people's questions.

The process of selecting discussion table topics, often with accompanying quotes, has become an important part of my spiritual practice. What leadings am I experiencing? In the midst of one disaster, it came to me to help the meeting seek God and find solace with a quote from Psalm 44 (MSG):

Get up, GOD! Are you going to sleep all day?
  Wake up! Don't you care what happens to us? . . .
Why pretend things are just fine with us? . . .
Get up and come to our rescue.
  If you love us so much, Help us!

Almost a year after I started the discussion table, an email arrived from Kim Lacey, the Ministry and Oversight clerk of Central Coast Friends Meeting in San Luis Obispo, asking if I might lead a program at their upcoming retreat to help them deepen their spiritual sharing. Kim is a former member of San Francisco Friends Meeting, where years earlier she had co-led a spiritual friendships program I had created. She labeled her email "Hello! (Out of the Blue)"—but, to me, her request did not seem out of the blue. Rather, it was in keeping with the work I had been doing. I asked Stephen Matchett to serve as my elder as I prepared for the weekend. I began the work of asking Kim and other members of her meeting questions would help me understand that meeting's needs. Because Stephen could not attend the weekend itself, I needed another elder. I was somehow drawn to Ann Marie Snell but reluctant to ask her because she was clerk of San Francisco Friends Meeting and the Central Coast retreat conflicted with San Francisco's meeting for business. Stephen encouraged me to trust the nudge to ask Ann Marie; she accepted, and our work together was fruitful. As I write this, it is almost two years since that email arrived from Kim, and Ann Marie and Stephen continue to meet regularly with me as a support committee to help me discern and obey God's guidance. In this shelter-at-home time during the pandemic, I am seeking ways to continue the substance of my work when the form has been taken away.

Chapter 6

The Elder's Work: Frameworks for Practice and Understanding

In the previous chapter, we looked in some detail at what elders do. In this chapter, through two frameworks, we explore how the work of elders might be practiced in our meetings. These frameworks are not the only way to talk about elders' work. They are useful as a structure, and they may also set your imagination on a path to explore your own travels in meeting for worship—to invite the elder part of you and Spirit to reveal how you might be helpful to your meeting in tending to the Spirit in your community.[1]

Meeting for worship and meeting for worship on the occasion of business are the core of our Quaker faith communities. Therefore, we will take some time to explore what elders might be doing before, during, and after meetings for worship and meetings on the occasion of business, a cyclical process where there is some overlap. This is the kind of eldering work that often goes unnoticed, yet it is part of the root system that sustains, nourishes, and strengthens the community.

Before Meeting for Worship

The elders of a meeting are called to attend to the spiritual life of the meeting all week long, in the days between one meeting for worship and the next. One very common elder practice is praying for the meeting throughout the week. This may mean praying for the meeting as a whole; it may also mean praying for individuals. The prayers may be simply holding the meeting and individuals in Love and Light. They may also be more focused, asking for divine presence and depth in worship and in vocal ministry. Additionally, elders may pray for messages that the community needs to hear and for hearts ready to receive that vocal ministry. Prayer is a vital elder practice before, during, and between meetings for worship.

Elders are often the ones who hold particular tensions or troubles within the meeting in the Light. They may also be the people who check in on or visit with individual Friends. This is not to be confused with the old idea of seeing whether folks were following rules or being Quaker enough. Rather, these visits—whether in person, by phone, or by video connection—are intended to lift up and to nurture the spiritual spark within each person and community.

At their essence, these visits are in the spirit of the traditional practice of "opportunities." These are small, impromptu times when two or more people fall into worship and share what arises out of the time. There may be a specific focus that is shared, but not necessarily. These opportunities can happen anywhere, any time—even during a social gathering, such as before attending a movie, a protest rally, a book signing, or a yard cleaning. These are not necessarily seen as spiritual activities, and yet they are sacred and perhaps are a part of a communal leading for us to see all of life as sacred. If so, that calls for companionship much beyond the designated time on First Day when Quakers gather as a body. Elders are typically the Friends who can be counted on to nurture the community in this way.

It is incumbent on elders to be personally well prepared for worship. This means in large part being disciplined and faithful to the spiritual practices that give them life and aid in their work in the meeting community. Spiritual disciplines, as noted in an earlier chapter, can take many forms; they deepen the elder's spirit and strengthen communion with Spirit and the meeting. The many practices that elders have integrated into their daily lives allow them to ground and gather those assembled for worship.

During Meeting for Worship

In meeting for worship, elders seek a deeper and deeper connection with the Divine, both alone and with the gathered community. Some people can palpably feel this grounding, this deep connection to the Source. While many elders are aware of and intentional about being a grounded and grounding presence, some who are very adept at this are unaware that they are doing it and do not realize how much it contributes to the depth of the meeting for worship. It is important for this to be named and supported by other elders.

The elders in a meeting also intentionally hold vocal ministry as it arises, is delivered, and is received by those gathered. In particularly deep meetings for worship, experienced elders watch for those who may be experiencing what appears to be spiritual distress. This spiritual distress may be evidenced by quaking, rocking, tears, or other signs. Discernment is needed when noticing signs of spiritual distress. Quite often, when people see quaking, crying, and other such signs, they make assumptions about what is happening. So, what looks like distress may in fact be evidence of a strong movement of the Spirit; it doesn't necessarily mean something is wrong or needs to be fixed or stopped. It may be something that simply needs tending. Or, the signs may indicate actual distress that calls for discernment about whether it is emotional distress, the work of the Adversary, or something else. The outward signs can have different meanings, and elders need to be alert to this and respond accordingly by listening and discerning and learning along the way.

Sometimes people drop to a deep place in worship, and it may be hard for them to surface after meeting for worship. This may include ministers who have given particularly deep and faithful ministry or ministry that the body has a hard time hearing. The energy dissonance in the strong connection between the minister and what was given them to speak and the resistance in the body may be felt by many. How these feelings and experiences are interpreted or expressed may look like confusion, or fear, or defiance, or anger, or acceptance and gratitude that a truth has been spoken. The consequence is that the minister and others may be left with a sense of disquiet and disequilibrium. There may be a need for a time of transition after worship.

It helps when elders notice this and make space for people to decompress. It may be in the form of a wise elder's ear to help an individual or community find a deep truth within themselves. It may be one of the things an elder tends to in the week or weeks following. An elder might also be given words to name the condition of the meeting before meeting is closed or in the period of announcements or afterthoughts that many of our meetings have. An elder may also suggest some extra time in the sacred silence to hold and perhaps integrate what has happened. In each of these situations, elders experienced in spiritual accompaniment will know how to be with people and the community in a way that is nourishing to all.

Tangentially, we note that some people attend meeting for worship explicitly so that meeting for worship will ground them while they do astral travel of some variety—for example, helping people who are dying or some other nonphysical spiritual work. This is important work that some are drawn to, yet it can take a spiritual toll on meeting for worship unless it is specifically grounded by elders. In this situation, the work of the elder is to guide the people doing such work in learning strong enough practices to ground themselves. Some elders would be pleased to help ground such work in meeting for worship and at other times, if explicitly asked. This is a better practice than using the meeting's spiritual bank account without the meeting's permission.

After Meeting for Worship

At the rise of meeting, elders are aware of the spiritual tending that may be needed. For example, they may make a connection with someone whose vocal offering wasn't as seasoned or faithful as it might have been. The intent here is not to criticize but to explore with the person. What felt rich and rightly led? What did their discernment feel like to stand and speak? An elder will offer queries, not judgment.

Some people experience deep and breathtaking encounters with the Divine during meeting for worship. This may be a wonderful mountaintop experience of light and glory. It could also be a much harder, yet still awesome, experience of being shown where they are out of alignment with God and good order and in need of a course correction. Some elders may be able to cocoon such an individual in the moment, protecting them from the typical after-meeting energy and the onslaught of the after-meeting chatter. Over time, the elder can help the person regain a sense of equilibrium in the new faithful place where they find themselves.

In between meetings for worship, elders often check in with each other for support and discernment. They may also find times in the week to worship together. In this way, elders become part of the spiritual network that holds a meeting together in faithfulness.

Elders also name spiritual gifts they encounter in the meeting—not just vocal ministry, which is what has traditionally been named and even recorded in our meetings, but the wide array of gifts that Spirit bestows on us, including those spiritual gifts that may look very secular. One example is the duties of the treasurer. Some people do these duties out of a strong sense of leading, seeing them as a spiritual service that they are equipped to offer. When this happens, the spiritual impact on the body is profound, helping the community to put God first while pointing the community to the spiritual dimensions of its collective dollars.

Although tending to the physical and material needs within a meeting is also important, this is not typically the work of elders. Traditionally, overseers cared for these physical needs, sometimes now called pastoral care among Friends. Elders are given the work of tending to the spiritual needs, which are often less visible and less acknowledged than physical needs. Many times, there is overlap between physical and spiritual needs, so it is good for elders and pastoral care givers to work in tandem.

Meeting for Worship on the Occasion for Business

Like meeting for worship, meeting for worship on the occasion of business calls some elders into different roles. Many clerks meet privately with one or more elders to prepare the clerk mentally and spiritually, to season the agenda and business items, and to set the spiritual tone for the meeting. More and more, meetings have named people—elders—to hold the meeting in prayer while meeting for business is in session. This is more visible than it used to be, but there have always been elders, named or not, who have practiced holding business sessions in depth and prayer.

Elders are often the people who can consistently name and voice the sense of the meeting. They are also the ones who can and do voice hard truths during business sessions. Some have the gift of being able to voice the hard truth in ways that the collected body can hear and take in without judgment, anger, or feeling condemned. They can speak with love and respect without diluting the truth. They often debrief after the meeting for business, elders with each other and elders with the clerk. When the meeting for business has gone off the rails, the elders will help the meeting work toward understanding and a faithful way forward.

Reflection on Eldering

In my journal, I made a small pencil sketch of what I'd experienced during the last evening of business at yearly meeting sessions one year. At the bottom is shiny dark ground, drawn in heavy pencil, and there is gray above the ground except for a vertical column of light in the gray. I'd labeled this as a distant pillar of light shining in or through a cloud of confusion, chaos, and doubt. I noted the ground was deep oily black, like blood or crude oil—a pool of self-loathing. A few days later, after reflecting further on the experience, I added to the sketch a small tiny white circle under the ground—an infinite seed of golden light and love that appeared deep under and within the darkness.

I don't recall the particularities of the business that night. I just remember I felt I'd gone into this really deep, dark place where I was standing facing a column of light and seeing the light, the gray mist, the black ground, all three, and just holding all of that.

After the meeting closed, a friend noticed I was in some distress and quietly came over to stand behind me with her hands on my shoulders. This human touch was deeply comforting.

Looking back, I believe there was distrust among those gathered and also a lack of clarity concerning the business being considered; money was involved.

Threads of decades-old controversy and conflict wove through beneath the surface. At the same time, there was light at the core, and light leading the way.

Janet Gibian Hough
Cobscook Friends Meeting, Whiting, Maine

Anchor Committees

Those in the meeting who have specific gifts and leadings may have an anchor committee or a care and accountability committee. Elders will often be on these committees, caring for the minister, the one who is carrying the leading, and also caring for the ministry and its faithful execution. This kind of care is appropriate at all stages in the life of a ministry: the conception stage, the stage of faithfully responding to the leading and acting on it in the world; and the stage of letting go and laying down a ministry.

Children in the Meeting

Children deserve the spiritual care of elders. Gifts in many children, some very young, become evident to those who know how to read the signs. Like those mythical kindergarten teachers spoken about earlier, elders can discern leadings in youngsters. Some children are natural organizers. Others take leadership roles almost from the beginning. Those that have a caretaker bent, or listen others into being, have those tendencies early on. Some are baby elders. The children themselves know this about each other, and sometimes they know it about themselves.

Intentionally nurturing these nascent gifts as a movement toward building the spiritual community of tomorrow is not something most of us are well schooled in. In this individual-focused Western society we inhabit, supporting community-building as a spiritual practice is very countercultural. It is good and right for older elders to adopt a much younger elder and spend time with them. Both parties will be enriched in the process, each teaching the other. It may surprise some Friends to know that those in the younger age groups have shown that they have a good grasp of the roles, responsibilities, and gifts that elders bring to the faith community.

However you name your grade school, middle school, high school, and young adult Friends, everyone who is concerned about their meeting should be engaged in meaningful ways with the young Friends, not just in intergenerational activities but as Friends who are engaging with the important issues in life. Many young people are eager for one-on-one conversations about their spiritual lives and experiences.

Reflection on Eldering

The most excellent piece of eldering I've encountered took place . . . in our small meeting house in New York State. On this Sunday morning the building felt full—30 or 35 people, children and adults. Friends had gathered and were settled for worship. Soon a little 2-year-old began chattering. It began to appear that she was not going to stop. Finally her older brother, 6 or 7 years old, said to her, in a kindly and friendly voice, "Katherine, the Meeting needs silence." And she gave it to us. It was the sort of quiet we always aspire to, comfortable, expectant, grateful, healing.[2]

Mary Foster Cadbury
Bulls Head-Oswego Friends Meeting, New York

The Sacred Spiral

We are all being pulled toward God. Some of us are aware of our yearning and desire to know more fully than ever we can the Holy One—however we may name that Sacred Presence. We may get distracted, for a minute or a decade, and then at some point our desire brings us back to our seeking. As Augustine of Hippo said, "Thou has made us for thyself, O Lord, and our heart is restless until it finds rest in thee."[3]

For some souls, this seeking leads them to the Religious Society of Friends and the waiting, expectant worship that is foundational to many of our meetings for worship. Waiting worship for some can be a time of finding a quiet respite from their busy lives and noisy world. Some worshippers find a greater connection to Spirit in our communal worship than can be achieved alone—a connection with our core open to conversion by the Holy Spirit. The distance between these two experiences can seem vast, or it can be as unnoticed as a breath.

At times, Quakers have had an aversion, or even an unspoken taboo, to talking specifically about our individual experiences in waiting worship. In that notable absence, it can be difficult to know how to accompany, encourage, support, deepen, and enrich each other's worship experience. In the absence of sharing with each other our worship experiences, it can also be hard to know the next step the Divine is inviting people to explore.

Given this, it is time to look at another framework, a spiral, to look at where people might be situated spiritually in a given meeting for worship and what the work of the elders might be, depending on the condition of individual worshipers. It is a way of recognizing that Friends come to worship in various states and conditions. All are welcome and beloved, whatever their condition. In nurturing and accompanying worshipers, what is needed from elders will vary.

We develop here the metaphor of a spiral to talk about where people are spiritually when they enter into worship, but there are many other possibilities. For example, it is common for Quakers to describe worship as "dropping down" or "deepening." Sometimes, people talk about opening wider or rising into the heavens. William Taber wrote about stepping into the stream. Teresa of Avila wrote about rooms in the castle. There are many metaphors for the worship experience, so if the spiral is not helpful for you, may that be an invitation for you to reflect on metaphors that illuminate how you experience and talk about worship. The examples that follow grew out of a time of worship sharing in a meeting in Australia that was focused on people's experiences in worship.

An example of a person on the first point on the spiral is a fairly new attender who is not able to settle his mind or soul or body. He fidgets, and he knows that he is being disruptive to others in meeting for worship because he can't settle his body. He speaks very tenderly about this being the closest to quiet that he can remember. His mind is normally constantly busy, but in the silence of worship the pace of his mind slows, which feels like a wonderful relief to him. This state represents what we might call the most surface, or perhaps outer, point on the spiral. This first point is a state of restlessness, of feeling unable to settle.

A person at the second point might, for example, read some Quaker history at the start of meeting for worship, feeling like she is reclaiming ancestors that she wishes had been a part of her life. In this, she is finding a different ground for herself. And then she is able to settle in her heart and in her mind—to touch that place of worship, that place of waiting in the sacred silence for the Divine Presence to be manifest. We recommend reading before meeting for worship rather than during meeting, however, for people who find this helpful.

Those who are at the most distracted, outermost point on the spiral need from elders a lot of compassion, tender holding, acceptance, and the invitation to continue worshiping with Quakers, as well as instruction about how to still body and mind. Relaxation techniques, intentional breathing patterns, and guided imagery may be helpful. It should not be assumed that the person will pick up our ways by osmosis, though some will. They feel something and are attracted because some part of them resonates with what is happening on a deeper level in meeting for worship. Staying with an instructional, encouraging tone is important. A critical, judgmental approach will send them on their way with a missed opportunity to enrich their spiritual connection—and maybe the meeting's missed opportunity, too.

An elder might convene a group of those folks in the meeting who are at the first and second points, inviting them to share and explore what works for them and even asking what they think might be happening. This is not about how long somebody has been attending the meeting. This is about their experience during worship. An elder called to this kind of work is a very special person as it requires specific gifts of creativity, patience, understanding, and a great love for folks who find themselves in this condition. There is a lot of teaching that is required. Even though we don't have creeds, we do have practices and disciplines that need to be taught.

The third point on the spiral is the condition where the worshiper is most likely to be irritated by the person mentioned above who can't settle body or mind at all. At this third point in the spiral, the person is able to settle in and more or less leave their monkey mind behind; they get past the grocery list or the checkbook, sexual fantasies, or whatever other distractions come up. They are able to get to that place beyond their own egos to where there is more connection with the Source. This is a settled state, yet it is one in which people are still easily distracted.

For those at point three, conversations to explore what their experience is during meeting for worship might be helpful. This might involve noticing, for example, when the mind is full of chatter and when that moves to something else. At this place, the Light may begin to show the worshiper where they are out of alignment. This is not a comfortable place to be, and many of us want to recoil and avoid this very rich, wonderful piece of our tradition because it may not feel so rich or wonderful, especially at first. So, having accompaniment and reassurance that some discomfort is normal may be quite healing. This being shown where we are out of alignment is very different from the self-critical voice that many of us carry in our brains. This is part of what an elder will be able to assist the worshiper to sort out—the difference between the critical voice and being shown where correction needs to be made. The self-critical voice may be a modern phenomenon, but early Friends do talk about being shown a different way to live.

Some people who are more practiced in the discipline of worship come to meeting already in a worshipful state. They may be said to be at the fourth point of the spiral. Sunday morning is not their only time of quiet in the body and the mind. They are able to float past most distractions. They come seeking the Divine—or Christ Jesus, as it would have been said in the old Quaker language. Many Friends, including early Quakers, would say this place on the spiral is mostly below words. Often people talk about sinking down below words, below thoughts. This fourth point, along with the third point described above, are where real vocal ministry arises from.

Sinking down to the spiral's fourth point, below the words, time and space kind of evaporate and we fall into a place of wordless prayer. This is a place where many elders who are holding the meeting go. When Friends first go to this place, they often have trouble resurfacing when the meeting ends. They are not ready, and it can be disorienting. An elder can notice this and accompany them, providing a safe, quiet space for them just to come back, collect themselves, and avoid the spiritual bends that can happen in trying to come back too fast. We as congregations do a disservice when we expect everybody to be able to listen to or read announcements and enter into normal conversation as soon as meeting for worship has been closed.

What we might call the fifth point is the deepest or most inward state—a deep state of worship, possibly an altered state of being. For example, an elderly, much loved Friend described in worship sharing a beautiful image of being transported into an elevator-type contraption and being lowered to bedrock. When the door opened, there was a glorious cave full of golden light and warmth. It was magnificent, and she would spend the worship time in this place, this sacred, sacred space that she had never spoken of before. She entered into this glorious cave consistently, week after week, worship after worship. This is a description of the fifth point of the spiral. An elder might be able to draw out that experience and allow her to see what a precious gift it is to name and give voice to that kind of experience. An elder might also discern whether a sacred and precious God experience is not ready to be shared. Some of these precious moments need to have time to take root; talking about them too soon is like taking a seed out before its time so that it can't grow roots or like helping a butterfly to come out of its chrysalis, which kills the butterfly.

When people in meeting for worship go to spiral points four and five, others who are sitting next to them may feel a gravitational pull to a deeper place. Their worship is always purer and deeper when they are in that person's proximity than at other times.

Not everyone is able to be articulate about, or sensitive to, these energies. It can sometimes be frustrating not to have a shared language to express these concepts. Sometimes, the best we have is metaphor. Part of what might keep people at spiral points one, two, or three is the fear of letting go or of the vulnerability of connecting with the Spirit or even with their own core in a deeper, more authentic way. We all know that if we do connect more deeply, we don't know what's going to happen. For many, both the deeper, truthful knowing of oneself in God and the unknowing of where that might lead is a very vulnerable place. Part of the elder's job is to accompany people in that deeper knowing and the letting go and to provide an anchor to make that safe, or maybe not safe but possible.

The experience of some Friends in worship might require envisioning another dimension of the spiral. For example, Henry Cadbury (1883–1974) said that he "could make little contribution in the kind of personal religion" that many Christians experience. "That may seem the more remarkable," he said in an address to Harvard students in 1936, "since the Society of Friends . . . is generally supposed to be a society of mystics." He did not experience "divine revelation or immediate consolation . . . in any demonstrable supernatural way." Cadbury said that his own religious experience was "neither emotional nor rational but [expressed] itself habitually or occasionally in action."[4]

We are not commenting here on Cadbury's experience in worship, but we do know that some Friends come to worship because of their commitment to the Quaker practice of social action and may not be expecting or longing for an experience of the Divine. They may live a life of faith in the absence of what is typically recognized as experiences of God or mystical encounters. Elders must be aware of this and sensitive to discerning how best to accompany those whose faith is manifest in this way. Elders might, for example, shine light on the variety of ways to understand God experiences, perhaps reframing what spiritual experience is. Elders might also affirm a person's experience and understanding, especially if it is outside of the Quaker norm.

Although these spiral points may sound logically organized, the experience is fluid and organic and sometimes messy. Friends may cycle through these five points, or spiritual conditions, sometimes in one meeting for worship and sometimes over long periods of time. They may vacillate from week to week. They may also spend a season or more in each of these points. Any one individual may go from planning dinner to a deep dive into the spiritual ocean and being in the Presence and then back to being irritated by a fly, a cough, a sound, a smell. In most cases, no one elder will be well suited to tend to people at each of these spiral points; it is likely that different elders will serve most fruitfully those at one or two of the points.

Using the metaphor of the spiral is helpful when we consider that, regardless of their spiritual maturity, Friends may find themselves at point one or two or three even when they are well practiced in worship. Those who are steeped in decades of worship may suddenly find that they feel very far away and disconnected from the Divine. While this may look the same externally as the experience of someone brand new to Quaker worship, the internal challenges are very different and present a different kind of tending for the elder. This may include reminding the person of what they already know; encouraging them to be where they are as faithfully as they are able to; and having conversations about the rhythms and shifts of faith over a lifetime, knowing that this sort of thing is a common experience for those who are spiritually mature. The elder may also help with discernment about whether mental health conditions are playing a role.

It is important to remember that, whatever the framework, none of these conditions and spiral points are any worse or better than any other condition. They are just different, and a person's spiritual needs are different depending on the condition of their heart and soul. The point is not what condition people find themselves in. Instead, whatever one's condition, the invitation to both the Friend and the elder is to tend to what Spirit is putting before them, which is always an invitation to a more robust relationship with the Holy, to living a more authentic life.

In this chapter, we have shared two frameworks for thinking about what happens in worship based on our experience and that of other Friends. There are other ways, other frameworks, and other metaphors that illuminate what happens in meeting for worship and how elders might exercise their gifts. Friends are encouraged to imagine what these metaphors are and what they reveal about that which unites us.

Reflection on Eldering

My mind became exercised before the Lord; and under a sense of the great cause I was engaged in, my cries were strong to Him in secret, for preservation in the discharge of duty. When rising on my feet I felt it to be in fear and trembling; for while sitting under the renewal of baptism, I had to believe that the state of the meeting was very complicated. But it is only for thee to read, oh fellow traveler, thou who art able to do it, in a similar line, what it is to be so engaged, and how great the care and watchfulness which is necessary, even when under the holy anointing. The states of the people are opened like flowers in a garden, some appearing beautiful to the eye, and affording a pleasant savor; others of a contrary appearance yielding an offensive smell; others having little or no scent. To know how the culturing hand should be turned upon these, in order to help, is indeed a weighty matter; and nothing short of that adorable wisdom, which alone is profitable to direct, can accomplish it according to the divine will.[5]

Martha Routh, 1743–1817

Queries for Reflection and Discussion

- What do you see elders doing in your meeting?

- Has an elder of the meeting ever approached you? How was that experience for you?

- Have you ever experienced a motion or a spiritual nudge to elder? What was that like for you?

- Have you, in the role of elder, ever connected with someone before, during, immediately after, or in between meeting for worship? What was that like for you?

- Does the metaphor of the spiral speak to you? Have you found yourself on any of the spiral points?

Interlude 8

Eldering as a Decolonizing Action

Mica Estrada, PhD

Strawberry Creek Friends Meeting, Berkeley, California

The word "dominant" comes from the Latin stem *dominari*, "to rule, have dominion over," and can be understood as behavior or systems that use power to bend others to the will of the dominator. Domination can include bending people, animals, plants, and other natural resources to the will of a person or a people. In the United States, and in many other colonized countries, domination was a prevalent and often unexamined series of actions taken against everyone and everything that could garner wealth and power for the select few. The culture of domination shaped this nation and continues to be prevalent in actions, norms, and values to this day.

In some ways, Quakers have a very checkered relationship with the dominant and dominating culture. There have been times when Quakers chose equality over domination, such as when men chose not to tip their hats to people of higher status, or when they used "thee" and "thou" instead of "you" to convey that we are all equal in God's eyes. White women were considered equals in giving ministry. And the ongoing commitment to being pacifist is a stance against violent domination used to secure power. Decision-making based on unity is another counter-domination approach that Friends still use. We tell stories about Quakers who break social norms of their time by walking towards people who are different from them as equals, such as Woolman's description of his visit to Indigenous people: "Love was the first motion, and thence a concern arose to spend some time with the Indians, that I might feel and understand their life and the spirit they live in, if haply I might receive some instruction from them, or they might be in any degree helped forward by my following the leadings of truth among them."[1] We can read about how Woolman, even when he felt trepidation, ministered to abolish slavery nearly one hundred years before Black people were recognized as humans rather than property.

But, as Donna McDaniel and Vanessa Julye's book *Fit for Freedom, Not for Friendship* (2009) asks us to recognize, Quakers are complicated. Early Friends' support of "Indian schools" and their engagement in slavery are just a few of the ways that Quakers contributed to and perpetuated domination over other people. The role of eldering in the Society of Friends reflects this complicated history very clearly as well.

I have experienced eldering as the act of accompanying another with great love, care, joy, and spirit to "midwife" ministry for the wider community. The act of eldering, in this context, is the setting aside of personal needs for domination in order to be of service to another and Spirit. When eldering, one may be doing whatever one can to create a sacred space in which others feel greater connection to Spirit/God/Love. These practices of eldering can be described as an act of decolonizing because the action requires a laying down of ego-driven domination tendencies in favor of service, humility, and surrender to Spirit. This is the type of eldering that has the power to contribute toward antiracism efforts and toward the changing of the domination culture that perpetuates the colonized mindset. Perhaps eldering of this sort can even be described as a decolonization practice when elders make a strong intention to release personal agendas and submit to love and connection. In this state of being, an elder has no need to control, to be right, to direct, or to bend others to their personal will. Instead, they feel a generous spirit of support and care for the spiritual lives of individual people, the community, and the environment.

However, there is another type of "eldering" that exists in the Society of Friends that is perceived to be the epitome of domination, and that is when one "elders" another by shaming, correcting, or calling out another to get them to conform to a standard of behavior determined by one or more Friends. The eldering that comes from a need to control or from fear rather than from genuine love and care perpetuates the domination norms of the society and embeds them within the context of the Society of Friends. This sort of eldering is the most common understanding of eldering among Friends. When control or fear is the motivation for correcting another Friend, then true eldering has been abandoned.

Does this mean that no guidance should ever be offered? It does not. When an elder feels led to suggest a different way of behaving to another, there are two features that must exist to avoid perpetuating a domination culture. First, the person receiving the suggestion and/or correction from an elder should have given permission to receive this type of Spirit-led guidance from an elder or elders of the meeting. We could say that membership in the Society of Friends is a kind of tacit agreement that one is willing to receive nondominating, loving, and Spirit-led guidance. We also might want to be clear that this is true. Second, the person eldering should be able to speak without any attachment to how the words are received and instead should feel a sense of channeling the will of God and then letting it go. These two attributes take away the domination of one person over another and open a way for people to be in relationship with each other, both when uplifting and when refining the ministry that is coming forth.

Chapter 7

Traveling in the Ministry with an Elder

You [a correspondent traveling in the ministry] don't mention whether you have a companion in the visitation you are now doing; I greatly hope you do. Your readings in Woolman's *Journal* will affirm the valued position of companions in our history, and my own experience witnesses to the importance in so many ways of having a tender companion. That and a group of 'elders' to which you can be accountable for your gospel labors are to my mind the most important parts of any public ministry.[1]

Lloyd Lee Wilson
Friendship Friends Meeting,
Greensboro, North Carolina

This chapter explores the practice of ministers and elders traveling together in the ministry in recent times. The two "companion" interludes that follow this chapter describe the experiences of a traveling minister accompanied by elders in 2003, first from the perspective of the traveling minister, Christopher Sammond (interlude 9), and then from the perspective of one of the elders who accompanied him, Elaine Emily (interlude 10). See also appendices 8 and 9 for essays related to traveling in the ministry with an elder.

One of the most visible eldering practices among liberal Friends today is a minister traveling with an elder. Even though this is not the most common form of eldering, it happens more often than it did even ten to fifteen years ago. While it is beyond the scope of this book to explore historical instances of ministers traveling with an elder, we do know that Elias Hicks (1748–1830) traveled with an elder from his monthly meeting. We also know that traveling ministers typically had a companion with them. In addition, an elder from the visited meeting was sometimes appointed.

Quakers travel in twos because that is what the Bible suggests (Luke 10:1; Mark 6:7). The accompaniment of an elder helps the Spirit have more access to the minister because the elder can provide the sacred grounding that allows the Spirit to come through more fully.

Elders nurture people who are alive in the Spirit, and some of these people end up being traveling ministers. Elders accompany the incubation happening within the person. Just like incubating eggs, you never know which will hatch and which won't. Incubation has to take the time that it will take. It cannot be hurried. If it is rushed, there is likely to be damage that could stunt or destroy something precious.

With this metaphor in mind, it may be helpful to imagine God as a brooding hen (Matthew 23:37, Luke 13:34) sitting on the egg within the person. Many elders accompany people who have something holy incubating within them. This kind of accompaniment cannot be done with an end goal in mind.

There are many aspects of accompaniment. There's the before piece, preparing with the minister. What often happens in the before time, especially if there is resistance in the minister, is a cleaning out—a spiritual enema—of resistance or whatever else is there. Part of spiritually accompanying the person beforehand is tending to this cleaning-out time with the minister.

Then there is the accompaniment during the minister's travels. The elder often sits beside the minister, or sometimes in the audience. What happens within the elder/minister yoking during this time is below and beyond the words. Sometimes the elder isn't even aware of what the minister says. When that happens, it is all beyond words; there are not words for that deep place, and often that is a place of deep, sweet worship.

Then there is afterwards. Some ministers don't have any transitional challenges afterwards, but others need recovery time. It is good for elders to check in with ministers in the days after ministry.

When people are called to travel with a minister as their elder, they have to do more of their own spiritual work. As they prepare and are prepared for a specific piece of ministry, not only does Spirit form the message they are to give, but Spirit also has access somehow to do deeper spiritual work on the human, thus forming the vessel. Elders need to be spiritually equipped to accompany ministers in this process.

Every elder traveling with a minister will have a different experience. For example, an elder's attention may stay where the action is, not going below the words. They may have a sense of being a worshipful presence in the group. When an elder feels restless or jangly, it is not necessarily generated from within them but from their feeling the energy of the group. It is important for all elders to notice their experience, to notice how the gift is expressing itself in them. This is part of "learning the vessel," learning who and what they are as an elder.

Reflections on Eldering

Given all the stresses and uncertainties there are for a minister, we can see that there is indeed a need for others to actively help to support, elder, anchor, nurture, and companion ministers, especially those young and tender in carrying the ministry that has been given to them.[2]

Lu and Kenn Harper
Rochester Friends Meeting, New York

As facilitator I have found I can go deeper into my topic, in unanticipated ways, when I have the accompaniment of someone who has listened to me ahead of time, who is listening to those present, and, who is listening for the Eternal. It is like the admonition: No Swimming Alone. Use the buddy system.[3]

Carolyn Schodt
Chestnut Hill Friends Meeting, Philadelphia

*****

Christopher Sammond was giving a talk at Friends General Conference. He assembled several people to be part of his elder support. I hadn't known him long but agreed to be part of the team. As I listened to him describe his process, preparing for this ministry, I kept hearing about various fears and his worries that they would get in the way of his leading. I offered to 'hold his fear.' He immediately said, "Well, you might not know what you are getting yourself into." I worried about whether I had been naive about making such an offer. However, what I discovered is that my fears and someone else's fears are not the same. It did not feel burdensome to accept that responsibility. Afterwards, he seemed relieved with how things had gone, and I think my role was faithfully executed.

Laura Magnani
Strawberry Creek Friends Meeting, Berkeley, California

*****

As I was preparing to travel in the ministry, I experienced powerful eldering in several visits to the home of Ken and Katharine Jacobsen in Delavan, Wisconsin. This helped me to clarify my leading to travel in the ministry and was a big part of my spiritual formation. They invited me for a *poustinia*, a Russian word, which meant staying at their home for several days of retreat, rest, worship, simple food, and prayer. Ken and Katharine were my elders in this way for several years. They had a powerful influence on my spiritual formation and travels in the ministry. I know they have had a similar influence on many others.

Chuck Schobert
Madison Monthly Meeting, Wisconsin

*****

Travel does not come easily to me. Deep roots bind me to my home ground, and each time I prepare to leave, there is a sense of anxious dislocation. There have been many prayers these past few days to detach myself from misguided agendas and the need to control events. Prayers to let myself be carried, to open to grace, and to accept the embrace of the Infinite.

An Invitation to Quaker Eldering

Elspeth Hull
Blue Mountains Local Meeting
New South Wales, Australia

In the early 2000s, eldering was bubbling up in North American liberal unprogrammed meetings of the Religious Society of Friends. Most elders at that time found themselves doing eldering functions without knowing why, or how, or if they would bear fruit. In fact, many were not even thinking of fruit. They were trying to be faithful to what was being asked of them, even if they didn't understand it or have a framework for their learnings. They all felt "weird" and like fish out of water. When elders encountered each other, they would exchange experiences, not totally unlike when queer folk of that time found each other. They shared their eldering "coming-out" stories with each other, grateful to have someone, anyone, who had similar experiences, piecing together bits of Quaker history that pointed to a spirit-nurturing concept of eldering rather than a punitive model.

Many elders at that time felt that people in their meetings ignored their gifts and sometimes even belittled, dismissed, or discounted them. Those with newly burgeoning gifts of eldering were up against the imagined elders of the past who had the reputation of losing their path. That ghost of elders past seemed to be present in many of our meetings where Friends, sometimes as self-anointed elders, seemed to have fallen into a powerful policing role to keep alive "what had been" rather than noticing and supporting what Spirit was calling to life. In those early days of the 2000s, many elders felt like they were part of a new incarnation of eldering.

Reflections on Eldering

Elaine [Emily] and I were settling into our roles as minister and elder [when I traveled with her in the ministry as elder in Australia]. The minister tends to the message rising within that needs to be liberated. The elder helps to draw it out, supporting the birthing of it in the metaphorical role of midwife. In this case, Elaine had words coming to her in the middle of the night for possible ministry content during the workshop. My job was to listen, support, and affirm what sounded right for this situation, offer any questions or cautions that arose as I listened to her, and continue to hold this upcoming workshop and Elaine in prayer.

We experienced an amazing nighttime phenomenon and have heard of other minister/elder pairs having similar experiences. I often woke in the night to pray for Elaine, including prayers for spiritual protection. These prayers seemed to help provide a safe container so she could sleep or receive spiritual messages. Night was frequently working time for both. We would learn in the morning that one of us had been up in the night and the other had slept. This seemed to vary from night to night. We often noticed that if one of us had slept through the night, the other one hadn't. When we are not under the spiritual discipline of traveling in the ministry, both of us usually sleep soundly. It remains remarkable to us that when this happened, despite sleeping so little, we still felt refreshed from the night.[4]

Cathy Walling
Chena Ridge Friends Meeting, Fairbanks, Alaska

*****

Guidelines for Elders Working with Traveling Ministers

- Protect the gift of the ministry and the minister. This is especially true for ministers young in age who have a big spiritual gift. People see the gift and tend to overuse it. Elders can help ministers discern when to say yes and when to say no.

- Help the minister guard against the rising of ego or self-satisfaction.

- Help the minister see that they must speak from worship and humility and grounding in the Spirit and not just from knowledge.

- Take care in what you say because many ministers will take the elder's comments very seriously.

- Know your own gift and stay within your gift and measure, just as you are requiring the minister to stay within their gift and measure.

- Keep the minister apart from the crowd, both before their session and afterwards.

- In the debriefing, ask the minister, Have you been faithful?

- Check for bodily reactions in the minister and tend to them as needed

- Watch for swings in the minister into serious uncertainty and darkness. Check in and notice what is going on. Do not try to make it better for them or advise them to perk up. Be a holding presence. Possibly suggest a therapist. Bring it up again at a later time. Often, people give big pieces of ministry on the weekend. They are in a high and glorious spirit. Then they return home to ordinary life and that spirit dissipates. Then, the Confounder may come in. So, check in with them a few days after the ministry.

- Trust the Light. Often you will feel what to say rather than know what to say.

Queries for Reflection and Discussion

- Have you been a participant at a retreat or presentation where there was eldering support? What was that like for you?

- Have you as a minister had an elder travel with you? What was that like for you?

- Have you traveled with a minister as an elder? What was that like for you?

- What do you find challenging about elders traveling with ministers? What do you find fruitful?

Interlude 9

Traveling Two by Two

Christopher Sammond
Poplar Ridge Friends Meeting, New York

In 2002, I was asked to give one half of the plenary address at the 2003 Friends General Conference Gathering. I had only recently held the question in prayer, and accepted, when I got a call from Elaine Emily, a friend from the Gathering I had known for a few years. "I feel led to serve as your elder for this," she told me. I told her I would be grateful for her support. Checking in a few weeks later, she said, "You're going to need more than just me."

"Oh, Elaine," I replied, "it feels like making too big a deal of this to have a whole troupe of elders—too presumptuous and precious."

"That's fine," she responded, "but you're going to need more than me, and I have made up a list three or four for you to consider to join us. Here it is. You sit with it, and we'll talk."

Thus began my education in how a skilled elder supports a minister in bringing forth what God is trying to birth within them. It has been a long, wonderful journey. And it is no exaggeration to say that it has been the elders who have taught me what it means to be a minister among Friends.

Before Elaine called, I'd had a little exposure to the practice of eldering, but not that much. During my first years as a Friend, I think the only connotation I had with the word "elder" was the finger-wagging, judgmental image of nineteenth-century elders reading everyone out of meeting for music, fine dress, or marrying out of meeting. My first inkling of what the practice actually entailed came firsthand. I had been worshipping with Friends for over five years when I was asked by Bob Schmitt, a member of my meeting, to hold him in prayer as he facilitated a day-long workshop at a nearby meeting. No one used the word "elder" for this role, but in hindsight that was of course what it was. (This was in the early 1990s, so I would hope that a newcomer to Friends might have a different experience today, but I'm not sure that would be the case.) I held Bob in prayer all day, concentrating for six hours on the Light coming to him and through him with a singular focus, which was a new experience for me. Truly, at the end of it, having focused intensely on someone other than myself all day, I saw clearly what an empty shell I was, without any real substance in the center. I would never have imagined that sobering outcome. What an introduction to the practice!

Two years later, Bob was bringing the keynote to Northern Yearly Meeting, and Jan Hoffman came from Massachusetts to serve as elder for that. She was joined by one or two others from the yearly meeting as he prepared and then gave the message. This was something of an eye-opener for Friends from the Midwest. We had never seen anything like that degree of intentionality in holding anyone in prayer, let alone several people doing it at once.

The practice of named elders, Friends with natural gifts and some experience, providing prayerful support and grounding was still raising eyebrows when, as co-clerk of the 1998 Friends General Conference Gathering, I initiated a Friend in Residence position to do just that for the Gathering and had an elder supporting me for the week. By 2002, when Elaine first approached me, the word "elder" and the practice it signified were a little more known and accepted, but not too much. I had asked different Friends to hold me in prayer and meet with me when I served as clerk of Northern Yearly Meeting, but we weren't very public about it, pretty intentionally keeping it mostly out of view. I wasn't just being modest when I tried to turn away Elaine's troupe of elders. I was reluctant to make a scene.

Fortunately, she prevailed, and three other Friends helped hold the process as we birthed that message. Over the next year I settled into a time of discernment, with periodic retreats to listen to what I felt led to share, and regularly checking in with Elaine. The others joined her in praying for me as I did so. Throughout the year, I prayed that what I would offer would not be merely a "talk" but the true expression of our practice as Friends, a Spirit-led message.

After a year, I had pages of writing, some of which had moved me to tears as it came to me while on retreat. Yet when I shared over the phone what I had written with Ruth, a trusted friend, there was a very, very long pause during which my heart just sank. Finally, she said, "What are you trying to say?" And I spoke for some time about what had been coming to me. After a bit, she said, "I think you need to speak this without a text." I was floored. It was three days before I was due to speak before over a thousand people. I had never spoken more than short messages during worship. My fears of choking and having nothing to offer loomed large. That whole night I wrestled with whether or not to abandon the crutch of a text. About 3:00 a.m., I relented, and surrendered to it. Immediately, a flood of language came into me, really phenomenal stuff. "I need to write this down!" I said to myself.

And it stopped. This was further confirmation—I should not read from a text.

The night of the plenary, I met in worship with my elders, the Friend sharing the plenary address time with me, and her elders. It was rich and powerful. During the worship, I prayed aloud, asking Jesus to use me as He would.

We were clear that the other Friend should speak first, and she did. When I rose to speak, the message was there, and it flowed. Yet as I looked out at the assembled Friends, no one was moving, not at all. They looked like statues, frozen. Daunted, but clear that I had only what I had been given and nothing more, I continued. What I didn't know until later was that they were transfixed, not bored. Unbeknownst to me, the elders behind me were visibly quaking in their seats. The room was filled with the power of God.

I got done speaking, and shortly after, I left the stage. As I did so, I broke down into a flood of tears. I could not stop crying; it was as if I had been ripped open. Elaine and the other elders took me to a back room and did energy work on me as I wept uncontrollably for a very long time. At one point I protested, "What the hell is happening to me? I didn't sign up for this!" Elaine calmly and gently reminded me, "Ah, yes, but you did," referring to my prayer during worship.

I tell this story in detail because it illustrates well some of the variety of gifts elders bring in birthing ministry with power. For starters, Elaine and the other elders held me in prayer, day in and day out, as I sought God's will for the message. I have had several elders who, once we were yoked together, would wake up in the night at the exact time I was up, wrestling in the Spirit, even if we were miles apart, and would hold me in prayer as I labored. These Friends holding me in prayer were a constant support to my listening and discernment.

Then, Ruth listened for where what I was trying to bring forth had power and where it didn't and named that for me. What I had written just didn't have it. But when she heard me speak, she heard it and named it. This is a crucial role of an elder as the minister is often too close to the content while they are listening and discerning to know where the heart of their message lies, where the power is.

Then, the elders took care of my spiritual condition immediately before the event, making sure I had had a good meal and was rested, and after that they supported the worship. They allowed themselves to be channels for the Divine to work through as the message came through me, all that energy literally making them quake as it moved through them, into me, and from me out into the room.

Finally, they cared for me, not only in the initial mopping-up exercise as I lost it but in the hours and days ahead, keeping track of my spiritual condition and supporting me in moving from the "mountaintop" back down into the mode of everyday life. This can be a difficult transition, to be sure. Being given a powerful piece of ministry transports and transforms you, and when you are done, the pieces don't always fit together in any kind of familiar pattern. It can be really hard to find the new normal, which is always larger and more faithful than the older one. The temptation to go back to old, more closed-down, familiar patterns is strong. Aftercare is not an afterthought; once you experience competent aftercare, some part of you knows that no matter how deep you go, no matter what risks you take spiritually, you will be nurtured and sustained in this new form and you don't need to fear jumping off the cliff.

I had a similar experience when Elaine and I traveled to Illinois Yearly Meeting in 2004 to give their keynote address. I was a little more familiar with the process of being yoked to an elder this time, a year after the Gathering where I had spoken. As before, Elaine had been holding me in prayer for much of a year as I listened for the message. This time, we spent a day driving down from Minneapolis to McNabb, Illinois, the perennial site of their yearly meeting. The leisurely car ride, with just the two of us, allowed us to catch up on many levels—what was happening in each of our personal lives, what was going on for each of us spiritually, and what guidance we had for the work in front of us. That kind of yoking time allows for the strengthening of a unique relationship. It has elements of friendship but is much deeper than that. Yoking together allows for the creation or renewal of deep bonds of trust, friendship, openness to Spirit, and a sense of shared adventure. It is almost like being lovers, without the physical component, for a discrete amount of time.

Once at the site, Elaine roped in some other Friends with gifts as elders who were also at the yearly meeting session, and we met in conversation and in worship in the day or so before the keynote. At the time of the keynote, the group of elders sat behind me as we entered worship, and I spoke out of the silence. Once again, the people didn't move while I spoke, though I was less disconcerted this time around. After some closing worship, the yearly meeting leadership told the parents in the group that they were at liberty to go get their children from childcare. Nobody moved. We went back into worship for a time, and then the parents were bid to go and relieve the childcare providers. Again, no one moved. We went into worship yet again. Finally, forty-five minutes after the initial worship was declared over, the parents left. One told Elaine later, "We couldn't move. We physically could not move."

Unlike the time a year before, I didn't melt down afterwards and did not need quite so much aftercare. I did need accompaniment to come down off the mountaintop, and Elaine and I did a lot of walking around the cornfields in

McNabb that night and the next day. Knowing I would be tenderly and skillfully attended to afterwards gave me the freedom to enter into a deep spiritual vulnerability, to go right to the edge of abandoning myself totally into God's flow. I was learning how being accompanied by a skilled elder supported deeper faithfulness in listening for, and delivering, a message.

After the yearly meeting, we drove back together. This drive allowed for the letting go of the yoking. It's hard to do at times. The spiritual intimacy is powerful and nourishing, not something that I find easy to just turn off or release. Having a day to do so made it easier as we gradually shifted more into our relationship as friends and less as partners in ministry.

The experiences of the Friends General Conference plenary and the Illinois Yearly Meeting keynote left me with no shadow of a doubt as to whether I would travel with an elder in the future. And shortly after that yearly meeting, I began my service as New York Yearly Meeting's general secretary, a main focus of which was traveling to visit monthly meetings. Over the years I made over three hundred such visits, and except for rare times when I could not find a Friend with gifts as an elder to serve with me, I was accompanied by an elder from the quarter or region of the monthly meeting or worship group we were visiting.

This gave me the unique opportunity to work with a large number of Friends with a variety of gifts that tend to be lumped together under the rubric of "elder." Over time, I learned who had greater strengths in which gifts and would try to match the particular gifts of the elder with the needs of the service we were about to do. Here are some of the gifts I would distinguish as being carried in different measure by different Friends:

- Helping to draw out a message: A lot of the time, when a minister is laboring with what they feel called to say, multiple threads come forward at one time, and individual discernment is not enough to sort through what has the most Power and Life. The presence in deep grounding that an elder provides, along with questions about content, can help the minister to become clearer in what needs to be said. Ruth's question of "What are you trying to say?" was such a question, and her observation that when I spoke without the burden of a text the Life came through is an example of this kind of gift. Another would be an elder who is so deeply yoked to the minister that they are awake with them in the middle of the night; when the minister is in a time of discernment, the elder is, too. Yoking is not merely metaphor; it is a spiritual, almost physical, reality.

- Accompaniment: This is the best word I can come up with to describe the kind of being with, the being present in depth and grounding, in the process of journeying with someone who is carrying a message or a ministry. It is a ministry of presence rather than of action, and it helps the minister to shift into a place where they are more able physically and spiritually to be a channel for the Divine. Elaine and my driving to and from Illinois Yearly Meeting would be an example of this.

- Holding the body: I have found some elders to be much better at holding a body of Friends in prayerful grounding than others. It is a particular gift that can have a pronounced impact on a body gathered for a workshop, worship, or message. The elder is literally a channel for Divine love to flow through and out into the body, grounding and opening the group to Divine Presence.

- Holding the speaker/facilitator: Some elders have a particular gift for being a channel of divine energy for another who is speaking or facilitating a group. These Friends have reported the experience of seeing and/or feeling huge amounts of energy flowing from a Source beyond themselves and into and through the speaker. Elaine and the other elders quaking as I spoke the Friends General Conference plenary message would be an example of that.

- Holding the room: This is a little different than holding the body. When a group of elders supporting me in bringing the 2007 Friends General Conference Bible Half Hours would come to center into prayer fifteen minutes before Friends started arriving, many of those arriving commented on the palpable sensation of walking into something when entering the room, which was half the size of a gym. Powerfully moved by what they felt upon entering, they asked, "How long have you been here holding the space in prayer?" and when they were told it had only been fifteen minutes, they were astonished.

- Discerning the spiritual gifts of others: Some Friends have the gift of being able to see the spiritual gifts of others, even if those gifts are latent and the person carrying them is not conscious of them. This is another capacity I would lump under the rubric of "elder," and Friends with this particular gift are invaluable to a meeting's nominating committee, using appointments to draw out and support gifts that benefit the whole community.

- Being spiritually present in the midst of conflict: A few Friends I have worked with have had the self-understanding of being called to help bodies of Friends to become conscious of hidden conflict and other unresolved disharmonies in their community's system and to be a vehicle for the shedding of those toxic elements. When I was called upon to visit a community I knew was suffering from open or unacknowledged conflict, I would ask these Friends to join me. What was hidden would always come forward when these Friends were around.

Interlude 10

Accompanying Traveling Minister Christopher Sammond as an Elder

Elaine Emily

Strawberry Creek Friends Meeting, Berkeley, California

In 2002, I was in Arizona at a Word and World Gathering, an interfaith conference, as part of the organizing team. I was busy from early morning to late at night with healing sessions as well as logistical duties. In the midst of the heat and excitement of all that was happening, I kept getting an internal message to call Christopher, a Quaker friend who was not someone I kept in constant contact with at the time. I did not know why I needed to call him; I did not know that Friends General Conference had asked him to speak at the 2003 Gathering. Still, the nudge was so persistent that finally I walked down the road away from the crowd, sat down on a rock, and called him.

Christopher was high with the very recent invitation to speak at the Friends General Conference Gathering. It was clear he would accept and that I would accompany him as elder, even though I don't remember either of us stating that directly. Now, just to be clear, I had never accompanied anyone on such a journey. Looking back, I would not say I was making it up as we went. I would say each piece was given to me as the journey unfolded. All my healing work had prepared me to rely on internal spiritual guidance rather than on a cognitive understanding of what I was to do. It did not feel like traveling in the dark, even though I was unable to explain conceptually what I was being led to do. I prayed. It felt like a channel was open to Christopher. I would say we were becoming yoked. I would call him when I felt a message come to call him, the message clearer than if it had been on my phone's answering machine.

I knew intuitively that this task of accompanying Christopher was bigger than me, not because I was inadequate but because the Friends General Conference Gathering was so large and because big, deep spiritual shifts were required of Christopher so that he could deliver the message he was called to deliver. While reading a written message would have been just fine and good enough, it would not have had the power of what he ended up surrendering to and delivering. I alone could not have adequately nurtured him back to secular reality from the liminal space he had succumbed to so he could deliver the ministry. This required more.

There were four elders total. We did not have contact with each other in the year before the Gathering, yet we all prayed for Christopher during that time. We did it separately rather than meeting together for worship. I don't remember how Christopher and I discerned who the other elders would be, but we came together for the first time at the Gathering. I did meet with Christopher regularly by phone, me in Tujunga, California, and he in Minneapolis, to talk and pray. I was aware that, in between our times on the phone, Christopher was a constant humming presence with me; I was holding him, and he was never far from my consciousness. Often when I am eldering with a traveling minister, I know the spiritual condition of the minister even when we are not physically together. This was definitely true for Christopher in the months prior to the Gathering.

In that year, I also prepared spiritually to be as available as possible to Christopher and the ministry. I always have intentional prayer time for whatever and whoever I am accompanying. I also hold in prayer the body of people who will receive the ministry. In those times of prayer, I almost always see the body being moved by the message that is being delivered. It is like my prayer sees this; it is like a picture, but it doesn't feel generated by me. The feeling of being yoked is tangible. And this is more than just an idea. I don't know how to express this for those who have not had that experience. One way I have talked about it is that it feels like a magnetic connection. There is a pull, and I am very aware of that pull.

Interlude 10: Accompanying Christopher Sammond

Elders are often led to specific ways to prepare for accompanying a traveling minister. For example, I often abstain from alcohol and sugar when preparing to travel with someone. I know an elder who fasted on Thanksgiving Day as part of his preparation for traveling with a minister.

Once we were at the Gathering, one of the first things Christopher said to me is that he had to speak without a text. When he told me about his conversation with Ruth, an elder who was not at the Gathering, I was grateful for what she had said because it meant that I did not need to say it. In the days before the plenary, Christopher and I walked many miles together, talking and praying, talking and praying, with Christopher praying very intentionally to Jesus. I also did energy work on him. Most of this time was just Christopher and me, but a couple of times all the elders gathered with Christopher, including just before the plenary.

During the plenary, I remember quaking like crazy and not being able to stop. I did not want people to see it—but of course they did if they happened to look at me. Mostly, they were focused on Christopher. I am surprised that I can remember some of what Christopher talked about. That is not always true for me. I spoke recently with one of the other elders, and she did not remember any of it.

Christopher did have what some would describe as a meltdown after the ministry, or what might be described as a major spiritual opening, such as Margaret Fell's description to newly convinced Friends: "The Eternal Light . . . will rip you up, and lay you open."[1] Regardless of how it is described, it surely would have looked scary to some people. In the time immediately following the plenary, we elders needed to provide a prayerful presence around Christopher to allow Spirit room to work. What was happening did not need to be stopped. Stopping it would have been spiritual violence. Sometimes these so-called meltdowns come before giving the ministry and sometimes, as with Christopher, they come after. And they can be spectacular. I've known people to jump on beds, for example, and to yell quite loudly at God.

Being in this spiritually vulnerable place where Christopher found himself is more than being naked before God; it is like not having any skin on. Everything is too much—noise, light, people breathing, people expecting you to be able to function at a normal social level. We needed to make sure Christopher had enough of the right kind of food and that he stayed hydrated and had enough clothes to be warm. Often, ministers either freeze or swelter regardless of what the temperature is. We walked and prayed and processed. He tried to find words for what he was experiencing. We did lots of energy work. I know some folks might say that he was just being a drama queen. They haven't experienced such a ripping open, or perhaps they have had the invitation and have not submitted to it. This is going into the wilds.

During this time, I felt centered in that deep place in the Spirit. I wasn't assessing any of this with my social work/clinical skills alone. I drew on all the deep mystical knowledge that accompanies such spiritual events. This is true for me in my own experience of encountering the Divine in large, wild spaces. One thing I notice is that I never get scared in these places. I have also had the gift of having others seek me out when they have experienced such encounters. Typically, during the mystical experience there is never any doubt that they are connected with the Universal and Primal Energy. When people step out of it, it is common for them to wonder, Am I crazy? Am I mad? Am I making it up? Others, those who observed what happened, may question if it is a psychotic event.

I also had to tend to my own needs the best I could. Energetically, when I am part of a big piece of ministry, I go over the edge and don't even know I'm close to the edge until I go over. So, when I did notice my condition, I needed to say, "I'm done for now"—I suddenly had nothing more to give, and other elders had to walk me back to my room. In addition, I needed my own outlet to walk and talk and pray, both alone and with other elders, so that I didn't get overwhelmed and sucked dry. I needed to replenish my spiritual, emotional, and physical bank account so I wouldn't overdraw my account. The energy doesn't come from me; it comes through me, and I needed to take care of my own needs first and then attend to Christopher.

Christopher and I checked in a few times after the Gathering as this piece of ministry was brought to an end. I notice a shift that happens as a piece of ministry comes to an end and is laid down. It is part of the rhythm of ministry, the laying down of it as much as the picking up. What I notice about yoking is that, even when the laying down happens, I still usually feel yoked to the person. My experience is that once you're yoked, you're yoked. That is true regardless of whether we have another identified piece of ministry or not. This is true in my relationship with Christopher.

I have since accompanied Christopher on many other occasions. Because of the spiritual work he did in preparing and delivering ministry at the Gathering, and because he submitted so fully that first time, he did not have to go through such intense spiritual and emotional trauma again.

Chapter 8

Envisioning a Quaker Culture of Eldering

Elders and the ministry of eldering are foundational to the practice of Quakerism. The ministry of eldering has gone through many ebbs and flows over time. We want to now explore what a more robust culture of eldering might look like in our time. What we share in this chapter is based on the lived experience of those who have been exploring the modern expression of this vital piece of our faith community.

What might a Quaker culture of eldering include? To return to the metaphor at the beginning of this book, a culture of eldering may look like the below-ground neural network of mycorrhizae connecting and nourishing the spiritual community. Or, if we think of the mycorrhizae as a metaphor for Spirit, a vibrant eldering culture might be those who travel through the neural passageways and grow up above ground as needed. The primary work of the elders in such a culture would be grounded in the monthly meeting.

Reflection on Eldering

When the gifts of eldership manifest, people feel seen and supported on their journey; there is a collective sense of spiritual community; resources are made available to support the spiritual deepening; and the community can sense and move toward collective action. The faithfulness of the community is enhanced by the function of eldership.[1]

Anne Pomeroy
New Paltz Friends Meeting, New York

We have noticed certain characteristics of communities where a culture of eldering is growing.

First, eldering is recognized as important to the community. The ministry of eldering is broadly recognized as an important strand in the fabric of the Quaker community. Often, this recognition begins with someone in a leadership role making a bold statement about eldering by integrating elders into their ministry. This recognition spreads when Friends experience for themselves the gift and power of eldering. That experience can then lead them to want to share it with others in their community.

Reflections on Eldering

Eldership was seen as underpinning the depth of worship; the quality of ministry; giving a special quality to silence. The focus of elders was on the spiritual life and quality of the meeting for worship, elders quietly keeping the meeting for worship running, acting as filters.[2]

Jenny Routledge
Norfolk & Waveney Area Quaker Meeting, England

If an elder is beginning to suspect Spirit is particularly active in someone's life, either in a joyful or a troubling way, they may look for ways to visit with that Friend to encourage faithfulness to the Spirit. In many meetings, it seems that tending to the physical needs of the members is acceptable and encouraged. It may help to know that, traditionally, the overseers took responsibility for the concrete needs of the meeting and the elders for the spiritual. Of course, in the ideal, both cooperated, overlapped, and supported each other, sharing information and resources as appropriate. How might we integrate that into our meetings today?

Intentionality is another important characteristic of a Quaker culture of eldering. In creating and sustaining a culture of eldering, a faith community should be intentional about it. Eldering is embedded in the structures of the meeting. It is not just ministers and elders who are intentional but also others in the community who recognize the importance of this ministry. Having regional workshops on eldering can be a good way to begin to introduce the concept of eldering to faith communities unfamiliar with it. Eldering is given attention and not just squished in among all the other things that need to be done.

Intentionality is important not only at the onset of the process but on an ongoing basis. The culture needs to be deliberately sustained or, based on what we have seen, it will likely diminish.

Part of how a culture of eldering is intentionally sustained is through elders forming community. Elders know each other and connect with each other for worship, fellowship, continued learning, consultation, sacred trust, and accountability. Though this connection may happen in a monthly meeting, it most commonly occurs regionally. This community of elders is intentional about noticing budding gifts of eldership and helps to nurture them along in either formal or informal ways. Elders also help Friends explore and discern whether they think they might be called to this ministry. As the culture of eldering matures, self-appointed "elders" of the finger-wagging type are no longer tolerated.

Some time ago, a friend of ours introduced us to the term "God-sipping." It is an interesting concept in the context of eldering. Even though we cannot find this word used anywhere, we like connecting it to what we know today as gossip. Of course, gossip is now seen as negative. Yet, in another paradigm, it could be seen as vocal sharing that holds the community together and builds it up. In its best sense, gossip—or God-sip—holds the community together because people share news as a way to support the community. This is not about confidentiality; this is about sacred trust. We share things that need to be shared for the good of the community and the individuals in the community. This requires a mature discernment, knowing what to share and when.

Sacred trust is very different from keeping secrets, and keeping secrets is how the idea of confidentiality is often used. Many people share with elders things that are to be held close. These things are tender, sacred; they're not to be shared with everybody or even anybody. These are not secrets. When secrets are the cultural norm, though, they prevent us from seeing and knowing what would otherwise be evident to us. Secrets prevent us from becoming our most God-like selves, living into our most mature beings, and giving our most faithful response to God's call, not just individually but also communally. It is important to not keep secrets because secrets are antithetical to good community and they often cover up significant harm.

Reflections on Eldering

As we increase our sensitivity and obedience in the eldering work that God would have done, we should seek the right balance between the need for privacy when an elder counsels another Friend and the need to bring a concern before the gathered wisdom of the meeting. We recognize that just as we have a corporate faith, we also have a corporate responsibility one to another, both to share our lives and also to be part of the lives of others. As a functioning body, the meeting steadies the individual, encouraging growth in faithfulness. Conversely, like the right use of any gift, each individual's faithful exercise of the gift of eldering lends strength to the meeting and to our ability as part of Christ's church to go forward in His work.[3]

Susan Smith
Rockingham Monthly Meeting, Harrisonburg, Virginia

*****

What I find compelling and inspiring about the lives of . . . early Friends is their mutual and active desire to be accountable for the spiritual health, nurture, and behavior of members, attenders, and the meeting as a whole. I believe we need to get back to this accountability and to revitalize the culture of mutual spiritual nurturing and care within our faith community.[4]

Margery Mears Larrabee, 1919–2008

*****

Another important characteristic of a culture of eldering is the practice by elders of communal and individual spiritual disciplines. Elders participate in disciplines that ground them spiritually and help them grow in the spiritual gift and ministry of eldering. These disciplines include communal and individual practices such as regular attendance at worship; a regular prayer or meditation practice; tending to their inner work spiritually and psychologically, including shadow work; tending to their physical selves in order to listen to their bodies as spiritual teachers; lives and livelihood aligned with what God asks of them; accountability in the form of spiritual friendships, a spiritual director and/or a care and accountability committee; connecting and consulting with other elders; and having custody of the eyes, ears, and mind (being mindful about what they listen to, look at, and take in intellectually).

Reflection on Eldering

> Eldership is all about love, but it is tough love. It carries with it responsibility and it can be hard. It takes time and spiritual energy, which is why care of ourselves is so important.[5]

Jenny Routledge
Norfolk & Waveney Area Quaker Meeting, England

Quaker cultures of eldering also need support, witness, and modeling from Quaker leadership. Since much of the work of elders often goes unnoticed, Quaker leaders have a role in bringing it into awareness by naming it. Those in leadership roles may also name elders to hold in the Light in meetings for business and for worship. Sometimes, Friends are first aware of the impact of elders when they witness public Friends doing their work side by side with elders. That may open their awareness to the elders in their own meeting who may be less visible.

Elders should be known in their monthly meetings. A meeting knows their elders, whether they are formally appointed or not, and at least some of what they do in the community. In a culture of eldering, language in our faith and practice books clearly reflects the positive role elders play in tending to a meeting's spiritual core. Nominating committees intentionally include elders, regardless of their age. In addition, nominating committees understand the gifts of the elders in the community and can discern where their gifts are needed.

Creative flexibility and spiritual nimbleness characterize cultures of eldering. If there is a culture of eldering that supports the emergence of Wild Spirit, the status quo will not remain. The balance of inviting the fullness of Spirit while maintaining communal stability is a tricky job for elders—and an important one. The community should share a familiarity with and capacity for spiritual wilderness. Related to the emergence of the Wild Spirit, in a culture of eldering there is a fluency in wilderness spirituality. There are elders to accompany those who find themselves in the wild places. Mystical experiences are welcome. Prophetic, edgy ministry is recognized and tended to. When the Adversary or a spirit of destruction arises, meetings address it with the help of elders. As ministers and prophets are called forth and supported, so are elders.

As with most authentic ministry, a culture of eldering is infused with moments of joy. Joy of the Spirit flowing. A joyous expansiveness. A lightness of being even in times of challenge and difficulty. Joy expressed in love for the community and all in it. This joy may be found when elders feel well used in the ministry.

To flesh out our vision of a culture of eldering, we now turn to three Quaker faith communities that embody a culture of eldering: New York Yearly Meeting, Australia Yearly Meeting, and Pacific Yearly Meeting. These are snapshots of a moment in time; eldering is continuing to evolve in these communities. In each of these examples, Quaker leadership—clerks, general secretaries, and Friends involved in public ministry—have been explicit in their support of eldering.

A Culture of Eldering: New York Yearly Meeting

A culture of eldering grew and flourished in New York Yearly Meeting, beginning in the mid-2000s, with the support and witness of Christopher Sammond, who was then general secretary.[6] It was an organic process, with Spirit moving through the yearly meeting as elders were named and supported in their ministry.

Christopher's experiences of working with gifted and skilled elders sold him on the function of eldering, so he did all he could to promote eldering when he served New York Yearly Meeting. He did not set out to create a culture responsive to eldering but sought to help the yearly meeting to reclaim a practice of depth and power, and he saw lifting up everyone's spiritual gifts as the way to make room for God to do that. He recognized that eldering was a highly important spiritual gift, central to helping the yearly meeting to ground and deepen.

When Christopher first came to New York Yearly Meeting in 2004, the word "elder" was not being used. But when he visited monthly meetings, he traveled with an elder, making a point of explaining that the elder was there to hold him and the meeting in prayer. When he facilitated a retreat or workshop, he shared that "the elders were working every bit as hard as I was, though outwardly they might not seem to be." Though people who attended Christopher's events were mostly not familiar with the practice of eldering, he rarely heard any pushback. He credits that partly to his role as general secretary and partly because people may have been feeling the positive impact of the elders.

Being accompanied by an elder who knew Christopher's gifts and could call them out when he lost track of them in his fears, he reports, was an "incredible blessing" for him in his work of visitation, particularly in the early years. The elders' holding him in prayer helped him to ground in the Spirit and to connect to the wellspring of the Source when opening to the condition of the individuals and groups he was with. The elders also served as another set of eyes and ears and empathic sensing when Christopher was trying to get a sense of the dynamics of the group he was working with, whether that was in an hour or longer adult education session or a weekend retreat. They also grounded the groups in worship and in the workshops or retreats that he facilitated with meetings.

In asking elders to accompany him, Christopher invited some who were not seasoned in the ministry. This gave Friends an opportunity to try the practice. In this way, Friends were encouraged in their gift and, perhaps, in further exploration and growth. A Spiritual Nurture Working Group formed and met several times for retreat and fellowship. The group also initiated ways to support the spiritual life of the yearly meeting.

Another way that eldering was seeded in New York Yearly Meeting was through a series of six workshops in 2006–2007. The workshops, held at Powell House, focused on nurturing spiritual gifts and included Serving as Elder: Grounding the

Life of the Meeting (led by Elaine Emily; Mary Kay and Janet attended as participants) and Supporting Gifts through and in the Monthly Meeting. This series brought about a focus on eldering as an authentic spiritual gift. One of the unanticipated fruits of the series was a group of more than thirty participants, many of them elders, who found deep spiritual community with each other. Christopher observed that "they had experienced spiritual depth together," something they had longed for, and they connected in that depth. Those deep connections supported the growth of eldering in the yearly meeting. Elaine was then invited back to Powell House to lead an advanced workshop on eldering, which was by invitation only. This workshop strengthened the community of elders and the practice of eldering across the yearly meeting. (Mary Kay was one of several elders for this workshop and Janet was a participant.) A second series of retreats helped to solidify and integrate eldering within individuals and the yearly meeting.

A year or two after the workshops, the yearly meeting began holding meetings for discernment.[7] These were a full day of worship in which Friends from every monthly meeting and worship group in the yearly meeting were invited to listen for how they sensed God being active in their lives and faith communities. During each day, thirty or thirty-five elders would hold the large group of Friends gathered. "The power in the room was palpable," Christopher says, "and the presence and function of the elders was made very clear."

Elaine and Mary Kay served as part of the group of elders for some of the early meetings for discernment. Janet served as an elder for the first five years and clerked the Meetings for Discernment Steering Committee for two of those years.

In these meetings for discernment, elders experienced and learned together what it is like to work with a group of elders—to be a corporate body of elders grounding and holding a larger body of Friends in open discernment. Different aspects of eldering were assigned to various groups of elders. Some sat with the clerk and some in the body. Some took on the particular role of shepherding, of welcoming people into the room. Some were assigned to the morning session and some to the afternoon, which was an unusual experiment at the time. In the debriefing, hearing other elders speak about their experience was educational and enlightening.

Having experienced firsthand how elders could ground and empower a body, several monthly meetings that were going through serious conflicts asked the body as a whole to hold them in prayer at upcoming business meetings. They also invited elders from within and outside their monthly meetings to come and hold them as they worked through their conflicts in different business meetings. At the subsequent meeting for discernment, those meetings reported back to the gathered body how they had found a way through what had been years of intransigent conflict. They gave significant credit for this to the practice of having elders undergird their meetings for worship with attention to business. This practical application of a practice that, from the outside, seems mostly mystical caused many to take notice. Having elders holding a business process really did have an important impact. The results were justifying the practice.

New York Yearly Meeting Friends had more and more firsthand experience of the impact and fruit of the work and ministry of eldering. As an increasing number of Friends experienced the power of eldering, more were attracted to it. Eldering began to be normalized in the yearly meeting. Friends in the ministry of eldering knew one another, connected with each other and strengthened their practice. It became common to have elders sit in front and hold the body in prayer during yearly meeting business sessions. Most retreat and workshop leaders at Powell House worked with an elder. Monthly meetings increasingly asked elders to hold meeting for business in prayer. The Spiritual Nurture Working Group of elders supported each other and supported the spiritual needs of the yearly meeting. The ministry of eldering began to thrive. Elders were tending to their needs so they could grow in their gifts and support their faith community.

A Culture of Eldering: Australia Yearly Meeting

Another culture of eldering has grown in Australia Yearly Meeting. Australia, like England, still appoints elders through a nominating process (rather than through recording, as with Conservative Friends).

In 2006, Cathy Walling of Chena Ridge Friends Meeting in Fairbanks, Alaska, traveled with her family to Australia to attend Australia Yearly Meeting. While there, Cathy noticed a wondering growing in her: Where were the elders? She held that question as she attended sessions. The question was still with her when she and her family returned in 2007 and she had private conversations with Aussie Friends with eldering gifts. Those conversations centered around the notion of eldering as being primarily about nurturing the spiritual life of a meeting and the individuals in their midst. Cathy also felt an internal nudge to elder during sessions, a spiritual leading that she followed, though it was not in any formal capacity.

The conversations that Cathy had with the Aussie Friends had a growing sense of life and spiritual energy and leading. That led to Cathy working with Sheila Keane (of Silver Wattle Quaker Centre in Bungendore, New South Wales, Australia) and Helen Bayes (one of the founders of Silver Wattle) in communal spiritual listening as they discerned way forward and followed the leading. Elaine Emily also joined in the discernment. The result was that Elaine, with Cathy eldering, traveled in the ministry in Australia to teach about eldering in 2008. Elaine and Cathy were not responding to a formal invitation, as Cathy writes in the Pendle Hill pamphlet *Spiritual Accompaniment: An Experience of Two Friends Traveling in the Ministry*. Still, a business meeting minute expressed that Elaine and Cathy would be welcome.

Elaine and Cathy's visit and teaching led to openings for elders to be more active and visible in the yearly meeting. One notable example can be found at Silver Wattle Quaker Centre in Australia, formed in 2010. The Silver Wattle Board instituted a practice of having a Friend in residence plus an elder for each course. A Silver Wattle Elders Committee called out, raised up, and nurtured the elders in various ways. The committee appointed an elder for each course, plus another elder off site to support the onsite elder. This was a visible recognizing and naming of nascent gifts of eldering in Friends and then a nurturing of the gifts with a group of more mature elders. That, plus formal workshops and retreats, educated and formed a group of elders to work together. The circle of elders began to increase and reinforce each other's gifts.

In such a culture of eldering, learning each other's gifts and supporting the strengths allows the whole eldering container to become stronger. Each person begins to increase their own gifts and each other's. Celebrating that each of us have different gifts and skill sets invites us all to lay down the dualities of right/wrong and better/best and any competition.

Since Australia Yearly Meeting is countrywide, these gifts began to move back into monthly and local meetings, not all at once and not universally. The yearly meeting began having Friends serve as elders to hold meeting for worship and meeting for business. Some people began to ask others to elder while they provided ministry locally. Some began to ask for accompaniment as they traveled in the ministry. It has been a slow and organic process. Many meetings in Australia continue to name elders. The eldering culture in Australia continues to grow into its own unique flower, one that will be different from any other.

In 2021 the Silver Wattle Elders Committee began an online Silver Wattle Elders Enrichment Program (SWEEP) during the Covid-19 pandemic to continue nurturing and educating elders while there was no opportunity on the ground. The program now invites elders from monthly meetings from throughout Australia to participate.

A Culture of Eldering: Pacific Yearly Meeting

Pacific Yearly Meeting has a newly flourishing culture of eldering, one that has grown in fits and starts. One start was in October 1997, when Jan Hoffman presented a workshop at the Ben Lomond Quaker Center in California on faith and practice at the invitation of the center's directors at the time, Walter and Traci Hjelt Sullivan. One of the participants asked Jan about eldering. Elaine Emily, who was there as a participant, remembers that the question gave her spiritual chills. From that moment, she and Friend Ann Harwood decided they would have the Southern California Quarter send a letter to monthly meetings asking them to invite two of three people—Elaine, Ann, or Kitty Bergill—to listen to meeting members' experience of the words "elder" and "minister." This happened at several meetings. There was no teaching, just listening.

At La Jolla meeting, Elaine and the other invited elder asked, 'Who are the ministers and what is their ministry?" They were able to name many ministers, and they had unity. One, for example, was named as feeding homeless people on the beach. That was when Elaine started exploring how Spirit was bubbling up in the Religious Society of Friends.

Jan Hoffman then returned to Quaker Center in October 1999, traveling with elders Kenneth Sutton and Bob Schmitt. After that trip, the Sullivans started naming an elder for every workshop given at Quaker Center. Monthly meetings began exploring what the terms "minister" and "elder" meant to people and noticing how ministry and eldering were bubbling up throughout Pacific Yearly Meeting. Then, in the early 2000s, Elaine led her first workshops on eldering at Quaker Center.

When new Quaker Center directors were named in 2006, the practice of having an elder at all workshops was dropped. Still, individual ministers continued to come to Quaker Center with the accompaniment of elders. And, though they may not have been named, there have long been elders active in Pacific Yearly Meeting's monthly meetings.

In addition to what was happening at Quaker Center, Joe Franco asked Elaine to accompany him when he was Pacific Yearly Meeting clerk. This was not named publicly. When a later clerk, Diego Navarro, asked Elaine to accompany him, however, it was explicit and public. The current clerk as of this writing, Laura Magnani, also has an elder accompanying her.

At the time of this writing, Pacific Yearly Meeting's Ministry Committee has a subcommittee on eldering, now in its fourth year. It began when the Ministry Committee (then Ministry and Oversight) began to imagine a way to support eldering and the spiritual accompaniment of clerks of major committees, intentionally naming and encouraging the task of eldering and noticing people who were drawn to holding the yearly meeting in prayer during the preparation leading up to sessions. Individuals had been led to do this spiritual work in private, each believing they were the only one doing so. They were acting on their own, not out of a shared public understanding that this was a valuable gift to the community. The eldering subcommittee has embraced these elders and their work in this ministry. For example, Pacific Yearly Meeting's 2021 epistle has a full paragraph about eldering and what the elders did during the sessions:

> The life in our Quaker communities can be nurtured by eldering and the process can be one more tool in creating sacred space. The eldering subcommittee of the Ministry Committee created a schedule of elders for holding the space of each meeting for worship or plenary, for each keynote speaker, the presiding clerk, and some other individuals exercising their gifts of ministry for our community. An elder provides prayerful and sometimes practical support. At an interest group, the subcommittee encouraged participants to practice this holding of space while a group of worshipers or an individual presents or ministers. Doing so helps grow the good in our meetings. Eldering can contribute to the work of decolonization in that the elder sets aside their own ego and their needs in order to be in service of the spiritual growth of another.[8]

At first, the subcommittee was informal. Elaine remembers that people pushed against it at first but then wanted to be on the subcommittee. The subcommittee helps provide elder support for yearly meeting gatherings. Monthly meetings have been asking the committee to do eldering workshops for them, which have been well attended. The elders on the committee have a group of elders that support them. There are now more requests for elders than the committee can fill.

Creating a Culture of Eldering

These are just three examples of where we have seen a culture of eldering evolving recently in yearly meetings that had not recognized elders for most of the last century. While there of course is no formula for creating a culture of eldering, a faith community can do certain things to make the ground fertile (for an example of such a process, see appendix 6).

To initiate such a culture, it can be fruitful to create opportunities for groups of Friends to have conversations about eldering and where they experience the impact of the ministry. As noted above, intentionality is helpful, as is the support of those in leadership positions. It is important to notice who the elders are in your community and to support them in deepening in the ministry. It can also be helpful to invite elders from other meetings to be with Friends who feel called to the ministry of eldering. Have conversations about eldering and how it might become more integrated into your meeting and the Religious Society of Friends as a whole. And, most of all, pray for the guidance of the Spirit and for hearts with the capacity to follow where Spirit leads.

Queries for Reflection and Discussion

- What do you envision in a culture of eldering?

- Do you see places where a culture of eldering is emerging?

- Is there anything you can do to help birth a culture of eldering?

Appendix 1

Four Elders Write a Book:
Our Process

Elaine Emily, Mary Kay Glazer, Bruce Neumann, and
Janet Gibian Hough

Elaine's Story

For over a year, I had been planning to accompany a family from California to New England Yearly Meeting in August 2018 to help with the children. When their plans changed, I started to cancel my trip plans, but I had a very strong message in my head to still go ahead and attend New England Yearly Meeting on my own. I argued with that voice. "It is expensive and I don't have money to throw away." "I don't have any reason to be there." Etc., etc.

When I brought it to my accountability committee, they confirmed that I should follow the guidance and attend New England Yearly Meeting even though I did not know why I should go. I submitted and continued with my plans to attend. Pieces of eldering work did present themselves as I prepared my travel plans. On the plane, I mused that earlier in my life I had attended Quaker gatherings that had totally changed the trajectory of my life. "Too bad," I thought, "I'm too old and settled for that to happen in this stage of my life." And God laughed . . .

Arriving at the site early, I was warmed and delighted to reconnect with a number of dear spiritual friends from my past and immediately connecting to some I had never met before. On the first morning of sessions, the first person I met was Bruce Neumann. I felt an immediate ease and sense of connection with him. He said he was the rising clerk, and I said I had been accompanying the Pacific Yearly Meeting clerk in an eldering role. The conversation, which was just beginning, was cut short. It lasted maybe five minutes. Worship was starting.

Two days later, when Bruce and I saw each other, Bruce said, "Elaine, in worship the Lord told me we should write a book on eldership." Hearing this, I immediately felt flooded with joy and delight and champagne-like energy bubbles throughout my whole body.

I laughed with the sensation and the ridiculousness of the idea. I don't write. I'm dyslexic, have ADD, and am totally ill equipped to ever even imagine such a thing! Besides, to write a book with someone, I knew I'd have to fall in love with them, meaning I'd have to fall into the love of God together with them. And I knew nothing about this man. I guessed he wasn't an ax murderer or he wouldn't be the rising clerk. But his being the rising clerk wasn't credential enough for me to yoke in this way. Anyway, how would a rising clerk have the space and time for such a project? One of the perfect, comforting things Bruce did is that he immediately took me to meet his wife Pat and tell her of the journey, as new as it was. Even though we both knew that our answer would be yes, the rational voices in us said we would season this, and stay in touch, and commit later.

Questions continued to rise in me. How could I, a nonwriter, commit to this? How could I say yes to someone I barely knew and say yes to being yoked with them for a very long time? Of the many nonrational things I have done in my life, this felt like the most ridiculous. I called my friend Mary Kay Glazer to consult and discern with her. She and I have witnessed and accompanied each other on many spiritual adventures. She already knew Bruce, having met him at a Powell House retreat. She asked, "Do you have an elder for the project?" I laughed some more and said I would talk to Bruce about it. Bruce and I agreed to ask Mary Kay to elder, to which she heartily agreed. She would elder as Bruce and I co-authored. We set a plan to meet via Zoom monthly for worship and a project check-in.

Bruce's idea was that he and I would each start writing, which he proceeded to do. I, however, was blocked with old "can't-won't-don't write" messages. I sat in front of my computer and, with a transcription program, started talking. I felt awful, a failure, unequipped, called beyond my capacity—yet even then, I never questioned that it was mine to do. I was so grateful to have a capable co-author.

Several months into the project, the three of us decided Mary Kay and Bruce would come to my home in Berkeley to watch videos of a small group of elders that had gathered to tell their eldering stories in December 2006 to see if there was material we wanted to include in the book. Mary Kay bought her plane ticket. Bruce, however, became clear he couldn't come to Berkeley and couldn't continue as co-author, though he would remain involved as project manager, a role he knew how to do.

By this time, I knew I couldn't lay this project down. It was on my plate, even though I still couldn't imagine how it would ever lead eventually to a book. Bruce had suggested that Mary Kay move into the co-author role, but that did not feel right at that time. As I prayed about who would be right, the name that kept coming to me was Janet Gibian Hough. I didn't know Janet personally very well, but I had been quite impressed with some of the pieces that she had written about eldering. I knew of her reputation as a deep elder for Quaker gatherings. Seasoning this with Mary Kay, Bruce, and others, we then invited Janet to co-author this book. She said yes, even though her mother was in hospice care. More than a year later, her mother died. Much of this book was germinated in that liminal space of accompanying her mother in the final stages of life

Janet, Mary Kay, and I spent time in Berkeley watching many hours of video from 2006 of five Quaker elders telling their eldering stories. In addition, Mary Kay, Janet, and I spent a week at Silver Bay in New York together and then another week in North Carolina after New England Yearly Meeting 2019. These were all rich, productive times in moving the book forward.

God laid this book on my heart even though I felt I was not a writer, and yet I had to admit that my name was on a Pendle Hill pamphlet, *Spiritual Accompaniment*, that in my mind Cathy Walling, not I, had written.[1] Yes, I thought I was vital to the process, and it wouldn't have been written without me, but it was hard to reconcile in my mind. One pamphlet had my name on it, and one book was being written that would also have my name on the front cover. Inside myself, I reconciled the ideas that I was an author despite not being a writer.

A naming from outside that corroborated that I couldn't write led to a painful spiritual and psychological process that was witnessed, cocooned, and accompanied by Janet, Bruce, and Mary Kay. Shaken to my core, I journeyed in memory back to the fourth grade when I was standing at the blackboard and being given a spelling test. A very mean, depressed (I'm sure), unskillful teacher ridiculed me in front of everyone in the room because I couldn't spell. In high school, I remember getting an A over an A over an F; the As were for ideas and content and the F was for misspelled words. I forgot the A and the A and took the F to heart. A lot of tears and quaking and worship later, accompanied by Janet, Bruce, and Mary Kay, I got to an "F— you; I'll show you" place. Subsequently, words have come easily from pencil to paper. I no longer say, "I can't write." I'm amused and somewhat stunned. Being part of a collaborative process has allowed a dormant part of myself to be reborn.

I still need someone to point out the direction. I haven't yet come up with projects or focus on my own. I actually think that one of my gifts is the collaborative process itself, which is what pulled me in the direction of eldering.

Mary Kay's Story

Elaine and I were having a phone chat—nothing unusual there. But what she shared with me—that was unusual, and exciting! This was sometime after New England Yearly Meeting 2018. Elaine started to tell me about the book writing project that she and Bruce were beginning. Yes, very exciting!

I asked her if she and Bruce had an elder for the project, knowing that I wanted it to be me. After she talked with Bruce and asked me if I would be the elder—well, of course, I said yes.

The beginning of this process goes back some years, to the already mentioned gathering of elders in Berkeley in 2006. I was thrilled to be invited to that gathering while also feeling unsure about whether I was really an elder; I was just going by what Elaine said, even though I had only met her a few months earlier. By the time that gathering ended, I was thinking, I am here because I am a writer; I can write about this. Well, I did write a short article for *Friends Journal*, but that was all. To then be invited, twelve years later, to be part of this book project was a joy.

Bruce, Elaine, and I started meeting via Zoom about once a month for worship and to talk about where things were with the project. When Bruce became clear that he couldn't be co-author, he suggested that he and I switch roles; he would be the elder for the project, and I would be the co-author. But, it was clear to me that I was not called to this. So, Bruce and I teamed up as elders and Janet joined as co-author.

The four of us continued to meet monthly via Zoom, with Janet, Elaine, and I meeting in person for several writing retreats. We had plans to meet in Berkeley in February 2020 for one of those retreats. The pandemic aborted that plan. Since we had the time already blocked off, we decided to do our writing retreat on Zoom. We met each day for worship and then spent several hours working either together or separately on different parts of the book, closing with worship late in the afternoon. This worked so well that we blocked off two days a week through December to continue this way of working. (This schedule continued for the duration of the project.)

In the summer of 2020, I felt a strong sense that I should offer to be one of the co-authors with Elaine and Janet. This sense of clarity grew as I worked on one of the book's chapters. Although the group knew that I was working on that chapter, I had not said anything about what I felt led to. Once that chapter was finished, I talked with Elaine, who quickly and easily and happily affirmed that leading. At our next meeting with Janet and Bruce, we talked about this, and the sense all around was that this felt rightly led. Elaine and I then had another conversation about how we would work together, knowing that our approaches to writing were fundamentally different. Janet joined Bruce as elder for the project.

And we marveled together that the sense that I'd had all those years ago that I was part of that initial group in 2006 because I could be the writer came to fruition in a way that none of us could have imagined.

Bruce's Story

For a number of years, I have held a concern for the practice of eldership within New England Yearly Meeting. I consider myself as having more of a "bent" toward being an elder than toward being a minister. Although Friends have occasionally named that in me and a bit more often named gifts that fall into that bucket, I have no pretense of being a "complete" elder.

The concern has grown out of an awareness that, without a practice of naming elders, Friends are reluctant to step into that role or don't have enough knowledge to balance a leading. Hence, some of the nurture and support that could be happening in our meetings does not occur.

My focus has primarily been on the elder within the monthly meeting. Various workshops have been held that focus on the role of an elder in relationship to a minister, and I have been encouraged that this trend is becoming more accepted. But my thoughts mostly come back to the crucible that is the monthly meeting. How do we nurture the life of the spirit in individuals, and in the monthly meeting as a whole? And whose job is it anyway? One of the issues with liberal Friends' discomfort with naming elders is that those who feel some motion toward eldership may feel shy about acting on it without some outward naming or designation. "Who am I to offer thoughts or encouragement to so-and-so?" I have read various brief articles about eldership that provide some light, but I have longed for a book that delves more thoroughly into the subject, something that might have given me a little guidance on my own journey or that I could refer others to if I saw the spark in them. But I didn't feel that I had the depth of knowledge or experience to take it on.

I met Elaine Emily at the 2018 New England Yearly Meeting at Castleton University. I had heard her name many times from various folks who knew her, and I had begun to have some idea of her stature as a knowledgeable and practiced elder among liberal Friends. And on meeting her, I found her to be delightful, and to have a similar sense of humor to my own. During worship in the pavilion on Sunday of that sessions, I was given a message (for me, not the body of worshippers) to ask her if she wanted to work together on a book on eldering. Her response was immediate and enthusiastic. Initial conversations there did not progress very far beyond both of us expressing how useful a book could be for the encouragement of Friends at various stages on the journey of eldership. We agreed to start talking regularly.

Fairly early on in our conversations, Elaine suggested that we ask Mary Kay Glazer to be an elder for the project. Elaine had had significant interactions with her, and I knew her a bit, so I was comfortable with this. After all, even elders can use an elder!

Early conversations focused on such basic questions as "Who is this for?" and "What are we trying to accomplish?" What emerged was a sense that, particularly among liberal unprogrammed Friends where there is no recent tradition of eldership, what was needed was a book that would introduce Friends to the concept of eldering and the different ways it takes shape (e.g., nurture within the monthly meeting, grounding gatherings, supporting a minister). Such a book would be an invaluable resource for someone who was feeling the motion of eldership but had no one to turn to to help them understand that motion. As well, it would be a resource for Friends who had begun to live into the role but needed guidance.

Beyond that, I confess that I had a hope that this book would increase dialogue among monthly and yearly meetings about eldership and serve as one more nudge toward wider acceptance of the importance of the role. I imagined it as an unofficial companion volume to Brian Drayton's *On Living with a Concern for Gospel Ministry* (2006).

At some point in this process, because of the responsibilities of being presiding clerk for New England Yearly Meeting and some complicated family dynamics, it became clear that I needed to withdraw as co-author. This was a big challenge as, although Elaine is an incredible resource about the practice and experience of eldering, she was uncomfortable writing. I had imagined that I would be synthesizing what we discussed and putting words on paper. When I needed to pull back, I wondered if Mary Kay would take on this role, she and I effectively switching roles, but she found that she had no leading in that direction. Elaine certainly felt that this was another example of God putting a sharp and unexpected turn in the road.

After some reflection, Elaine was led to ask Janet Gibian Hough to be co-author. I was enthusiastic as I know Janet well from our work together on the ad hoc Structural Review Committee of New England Yearly Meeting. It also kept the bicoastal co-author thing going, which I thought might give a slight boost to the appeal of the book. I was comfortable continuing remotely as an additional elder, with the idea that I might also at times put on the hat of "project manager."

At this point, I think the project began to pick up speed. After a multi-day in-person gathering of Elaine, Janet, and Mary Kay, during which they reviewed the tapes from a consultation with a group of elders, they began to gather a compendium of relevant materials to draw from, including transcriptions of various tapes that Elaine had, documents that various folks had held on to from eldering workshops, and articles from *Friends Journal*. At some point, a preliminary table of contents appeared (I think this was "given" to Elaine), and most of these resources were arranged into folders where they seemed to belong.

Some discussions were held again about the goal of the book and how extensive it should be, recognizing that there might be enough material for a second volume. The sense returned to the notion that the need is greatest amongst those who are just beginning to identify as an elder and those who are beginning to practice the art but don't have many resources to rely on. If there were enough material for a volume two, that could be considered later.

At some point that summer, I pointed out that, given the wealth of material gathered, it was time to begin synthesizing and writing. Although Elaine had begun to write a bit, she seemed unlikely to be the primary assembler of words on the page. At that time, Janet did not feel led to begin that part of the work, but Mary Kay had had some opening towards writing.

So, we found ourselves a team with a great deal of resources, a compendium of information, and good working relationships amongst us. And a book to write.

Janet's Story

For me, the invitation to join in the writing of this book began with an out-of-the-blue phone call as I was walking with my dog on a trail covered with leaves in the crisp beauty of a fall day in the Maine woods. I was ruminating unhappily on endings. The call that broke through my thoughts startled me. It was Elaine, asking if I'd be open to joining in this book project. I sat down on a log so as not to lose reception, and we talked. My first reaction was interest, which moved to excitement mixed with self-doubt. I said I'd consider the invitation and resumed my walk.

I had first met Elaine in 2006 when she came to New York to lead a retreat on eldering, part of a series of retreats on spiritual gifts sponsored by New York Yearly Meeting's Coordinating Committee on Ministry and Counsel. The retreat was such a deeply meaningful experience for me that I registered for the rest of the series (with different facilitators) and then for two subsequent retreats on eldering led by Elaine. I was always glad when our paths crossed over the years.

When Elaine told me about the book project, I felt a clear internal sense of "yes." I checked my excitement to consider whether I was simply responding to a human desire to work with someone I admired. Was I just wanting to be needed? Or was there a deeper prompting of Spirit—a sense of Way opening to join this small band of elders on this journey? I did not have a support committee or group of people I could easily call on to help me in my discernment. Instead, I tested out how it felt internally when I talked about the possibility of writing the book with others, noticing the feelings that arose— not so much what others asked or what I said in reply but simply how it felt to talk about it. I also considered how it felt when I thought about it, when I just was holding the question internally. The answer remained yes.

Elaine planned to travel east in early December 2018 for a gathering of Quaker women with a call to ministry. I would be there serving as an elder for the facilitators, so we would have time to talk about the book in person. Instead, on the first night of the gathering, my mother, who was 101, had a bad fall. I left early in the morning to be with her. My accompanying of my mother in the final year of her life wove its way through my engagement with writing this book—and on that journey with my mother, I was held and accompanied by Elaine, Mary Kay, and Bruce.

In early 2019, Mary Kay and I flew to Elaine's in Berkeley to listen to the many hours of recordings from the 2006 meeting of elders that Elaine had called together. In March, we spent a long weekend working at Silver Bay in New York, and in August we met up at Mary Kay's house in North Carolina. Over time, the outline of the book was set to paper—not by me but by Mary Kay. We planned to meet again in Berkeley in early 2020. Then, the Covid-19 pandemic changed everything. We learned the power of worship on Zoom. Elaine wrote page after page on yellow legal pads, which she read to us and we recorded on Zoom along with hours of deep conversations and playful banter.

I transcribed recordings, made notes, and gathered resources—but I was not writing the book. Why not? I could see the arc of the book and the detailed pieces. Why were the words and thoughts to string them together not coming? Unlike Elaine, I had had earlier experiences in school and work of being able to do this sort of thing. Then, when Mary Kay felt a nudge to start writing, I felt a degree of rightness about it, a correctness—sheer relief. I shifted into the roles of elder and of keeper of the files and notes and citations.

Looking back, these years of writing have been a time of upheaval and many changes. Our attention was drawn in different directions than expected. We have grown and deepened in different ways as we have navigated our changing roles. The writing has been like a journey on water, moving through the swirling nature of these times, blown onwards by the breath of Spirit.

Appendix 2

Eldering in Non-Quaker Environments

Elaine Emily
Strawberry Creek Friends Meeting, Berkeley, California

Eldering, as in spiritual accompaniment, in non-Quaker environments has taught me many lessons. Most of my earliest accompaniment was with non-Quaker social activists from other faith traditions. It was so wonderful to have these folks of faith name, recognize, and validate my eldering gifts. No one couched my gifts by saying, "Everyone has gifts . . . and so yours isn't special." They embraced everyone as having "special gifts." They also showed me what was expected from elders in a faith community. What a gift it was to me.

One practice might be similar to our practice of opportunities, which I'd never heard of at the time. A sign-up sheet would be posted in a prominent place with half-hour time slots so folks could sign up for private time with an elder to pray, request hands-on healing, or verbally share a burden. Folks would ask for prayers, not in a generic way, not sometime in the future when you get around to it in private, but right now, in public, with words, touch, tears, laughter, maybe even a dance—the full range of emotions, from a joyful celebration of the inbreaking of God's love right now to regret, confession, sadness, and remorse to bearing witness of connectivity with God. Blessing each other and ourselves was a communal part of the celebration.

I've accompanied mostly Quaker ministers outside Quaker boundaries. Having deep ministry laid on one amidst demonstrations is often a burden. Demonstrations are often loud, disjointed, well-intentioned groups lacking in deep spiritual grounding. It takes a lot of spiritual authority to command the attention of such a crowd and fold them into a gathered connection with the Divine. Having the additional accompaniment of an elder helps liberate the fullness of the message for those gathered.

Other unusual situations where I have accompanied Quaker ministry in secular settings include leading an international yoga conference focusing on the environment, attending meetings with college presidents to present radically inclusive educational programs for the most disenfranchised, and book signings. All of these were requests for accompaniment for what the individuals understood to be their ministry, what they were led to do. Those of us who take this work seriously don't have an on-off button. We become part of who we are all the time in all settings. Folks notice. While often it is unconscious, folks make remarks like, "Are you our personal pastor?"

Appendix 3

Working with an Elder

Carl Magruder
Strawberry Creek Friends Meeting, Berkeley, California

When I first worked with an elder, it was as the plenary speaker at Ohio Valley Yearly Meeting in 2006. I had been given spiritual eldering attention previously: naming of my gifts, naming of ministry, and personal integrity questions, both encouragement and pruning. This was the first time that I was being given a proper forum ("30 to 90 minutes," they told me!).

My elder Elaine Emily and I discerned a few key pieces as I approached the work.

First, I had been given permission by another of my elders, Bob Schmitt, *not* to speak. He pointed out that in the Quaker tradition I should speak only what was given to me or not at all. Because my topic was one in which I was well read, passionate, opinionated, and articulate, it would have been easy for me either to prepare an impressive speech to read or to improvise intelligently, rationally. We agreed that neither approach was appropriate; only total reliance on Spirit should give me language. This was liberating. If I didn't speak, there might be those who would question of even criticize me, but I knew that it was right for me to hold this possibility close and that there would be those who would recognize my faithfulness if this occurred. They would also recognize if I outran my guide!

Second, the ministry that I carry, the Gospel of the Earth, is apocalyptic both in the sense that it predicts the end of the world as we know it and because Old Testament types of disasters are the likely result of choices made every day by those who are listening. The message that the listeners' sin will result in devastating consequences is built in and scientifically justified. Amos and Jeremiah have nothing on global climate change. It is brutal.

Friend Muriel Bishop once said, "Truth without love is brutality. Love without truth is sentimentality." My goal was not only to speak truth with love in my heart but also to give voice to that love and to speak from a heart space. This is particularly hard for those of us who allow ourselves to live with the incredible precariousness of the biosphere and knowledge of the willful decisions that perpetuate this precariousness. We travel often in a dark country, and that darkness clings to our souls, our minds, our hearts, and our bodies. The pain that we feel can lash out at others, or scare them, or indict them. We have to do our own work of confession, grieving, contrition, forgiveness, healing, and repentance over and over again. This is not solitary work.

Elaine helped me with the process of getting my house in order. She agreed that if I was "in the trees" during my talk, she would stand silently in the center front row and I would stop talking instantly. This safeguard comforted and freed me. Kristina Keefe-Perry was also a part of my eldering team, and she agreed to hold my pain and my worry for the duration of the evening.

Our third determination regarded the source of ministry. When John Woolman went to visit the Indians, he used an interpreter for some of his visit, but toward the end he spoke from the Spirit without an interpreter. One tribal elder who did not speak English said, "I love to listen to the place the words come from."

For me, the words come from that deep well of Spirit, the Center, where language cannot exist because it is unnecessary and inadequate. I have not the skill to stay connected to that Center and simultaneously be at the shallower level where words take shapes and colors to form the patterns that I will speak, patterns not yet at the even more surface level where the words come out of my mouth and are received (though we are all simultaneously connected in the deep place as well). For this, I need an elder

I have worked with Kristina Keefe-Perry, Elaine Emily, and Valerie Nuttman more than with other elders. They were present at Ohio Valley Yearly Meeting, eldered for me at North Carolina Yearly Meeting (Conservative), and accompanied me during the Friends General Conference Bible Half Hours and on many other occasions. They have done the eldering schleppo work of bringing hot tea with lemon, and the scary eldering accountability work of asking me if I was staying out of debt, not drinking too much, maintaining integrity in personal relationships, and continuing to study. I have had complete strangers elder for me, and, by grace, that can certainly work. With established eldering relationships, however, there is an ease and a sweetness that allows me to sink right down to the bottom of the well and to open completely to whatever is there. I sit in silence for a quarter of an hour or more, waiting to see if colored shapes will come and dance around me, eventually forming words for those gathered. When the words are pushing me, I stand and speak.

My elder stays centered down, holding the connection open for me so that I can be in the place where the words are and still have access to the deep well of Spirit. I may speak a piece and not know what is next. I can take silence and immediately drop down and open so that the next part of the pattern of my ministry can find me. On my own, I may find a small piece at the bottom and bring it up—a two-minute message in meeting for worship on First Day happens like this for me. To bring a more complex message, I have to have the channel continually open, and I am utterly dependent on my elder for this.

What we found was that with the deep holding of seasoned elders, and the agreement not to let anger or condemnation form the energy of the talk, I was made profoundly aware of my own deep despair and sorrow for the Earth and for the tragedy of our human failure to understand that everything is interconnected. I was enabled to live from that place. For long moments I stood on stage silently, overcome with grief, tears streaming down my face, my voice gone. This was the ministry that was in me to bring—a broken heart, not a consummate intellect.

The fourth eldering consideration is the gathered body. Sometimes, if there are two elders, one may focus more on holding or grounding the whole space and everybody in it while the other focuses on the minister. I am reassured that an elder is monitoring the spiritual experience of the listeners, perhaps in a way that I cannot while I am speaking. I believe that the elder's understanding of the group's need becomes part of the spiritual mix and shapes and informs what is brought forth. This is another reason that I do not prepare a talk but submit myself to being prepared to serve whatever is alive in the space at the time.

Lastly, there is a debrief. This may start with an elder running interference for me after my ministry is done. In my fatigue, relief, and closeness to God, I am vulnerable to various missteps at that time. I am very sensitive to criticism or argument. I am susceptible to praise and admiration. I may speak not from the center and not in good service to Truth. So, the elder may make excuses for me and take me apart to walk or sit silently.

After a while, the inevitable query will come: "Was thee faithful?" I will take the question with me into the silence and really listen. "I was faithful, yes. I even said the part about repentance, which I might have been tempted to omit because it is hard. I tried a little too hard to lighten it with humor at this one point and had to recenter." The elder will nod or offer other insight. At a talk at Pendle Hill, my elder observed that the young people there might not remember what I said later, but they would remember that when I got to the end of something I asked for silence and centered down for the next piece. What I *did* was perhaps more meaningful than what I *said*! Elders keep ministers "low" by keeping the focus always on serving Spirit—on the message, not the messenger.

This is my experience. I have spoken to other ministers and other elders, and there are many different approaches, needs, risks, gifts, and methods. I like to think that one way or the other, the minister is going to conceive, gestate, and deliver the ministry and the elder is going to midwife in whatever way is necessary. Ultimately, both are focused on the miracle of the baby, but the interplay between them is deep, intimate, and very holy. Both have innate gifts and tendencies that they have consciously developed, as a musician does. The song that they bring out has salvific power.

Appendix 4

Holding in the Light

Moira Darling
Castlemaine Worshipping Group, Victoria, Australia

The experience of being held in the Light during a time of discord and misunderstandings in my local meeting convinced me I was a Quaker. Many years later, I realised it was the person I had the disagreement with that was holding me in the Light. It was an act of spiritual discipline and love that I deeply respect and aspire to in my own practice. Although I knew I was being held in the Light, I thought it was some quiet Quaker in some corner of Australia doing this for all Quakers. I didn't connect it to an intentional action directed towards myself, yet I could feel it.

Quakers hold each other in the Light during times of duress and debility, and many of us have felt that loving embrace during our times of trial. I recall the experience many years ago of being held in the Light following surgery. It was a tangible feeling in my body that I connected to the intentional action of friends in my local meeting caring for me. I learnt then to know consciously what it was to be held in the Light. Over the years, Quakers have spoken with gratitude of being held in the Light and knowing they were held from feeling the sensation in their bodies.

The healing power of being held in the Light is something we often speak about or engage in. Less frequently do we speak of holding each other in the Light as we embark on a course of work or engagement in the world. I learnt the power of this when, during a period of deep burn-out, I visited Friends General Conference in the United States to attend a course on spiritual experience (I want to note that I had committed to the course before I became burnt out). I had, with some encouragement, applied to the Thanksgiving Fund for support and been granted financial support for the journey. However, the most unexpected, and greater, level of support I received was being held in the Light by a group of faithful and mostly unknown Quakers whilst on my trip. On the way to the airport, I noticed that familiar feeling and said to my partner, "I think I'm being held in the Light." As I finished saying that, a text message came through from the Thanksgiving Fund Committee to say that I was being held in the Light. It felt like a miracle.

The miracle continued at Friends General Conference. The whole conference and venue felt like a crucible of love and Light. It was palpable from the moment I arrived. At the opening night session, there was a line of people sitting on chairs across the stage. When I asked what they were doing, I was told they were holding the session in the Light along with others scattered around the room. Being held in this way at the gathering and by Friends in Australia made the week at this conference such a powerful experience. I am usually extremely uncomfortable at any large gathering, yet here amongst 1,500 strangers I felt comfortable and at ease. Every conversation was important, and I was able to use my time well in both the formal and informal sessions. It felt like another miracle.

I have had other instructional experiences around holding in the Light. One time another Friend and myself were holding a workshop group in the Light for Elaine Emily. As the participants broke up into small groups, it was as though a wild storm erupted around and inside each of us. It took great concentration to hold ourselves physically stable and maintain focus on holding the group in the Light until they settled into their work and came back into the large group. It was quite exhausting and proved a lesson on how much energy and focus is required to effectively hold others in the Light.

Sometimes it happens that no matter how much we want to, we are not able or ready to hold others in the Light. We have to have done our own "inner work" to do this work. This was starkly brought into focus for me when I tried to support the work of the First Nations Committee at their first workshop with Indigenous and Quaker participants by holding it in the Light as an additional support. I failed miserably. As the workshop progressed, my mind was filled with images, remembrances, and connections in my own life and ancestral line that needed to be known and worked through in relation to our impact on the First Nations people of this land. The elder at the workshop, who was holding it in the Light, was a great support in helping me understand the importance of the inner work in enabling a deeper engagement with the spiritual work and providing a foundation from which it is possible to hold others in the Light. In subsequent workshops with First Nations peoples, I was able to contribute more deeply and hold the people and space in the Light.

One last thing to be aware of is the importance of a gentle release so the folks being held don't have a bumpy landing. I am sure there are many ways of managing this transition. I tend to tuck my image of those I'm holding in the Light into a pocket of my heart.

Although I have spoken about the energy, effort, and focus required to hold others in the Light, there are also exceptions. At one Australia Yearly Meeting I was called into a business meeting working through issues around the development of Silver Wattle Quaker Centre. This was very contentious at the time amongst Quakers. Even though I rarely went to business sessions, I was strongly called into the session on Silver Wattle. I found a seat in the room and sat. I wasn't called to speak. I just sat, and while I sat, I could feel a strong stream of energy entering the top of my head during the meeting. It was extraordinary. I stayed for the course of the meeting and was most surprised at the end of the session when the clerk thanked all those holding the meeting in the Light and looked straight at me. I was astounded—was this what I had been doing, while I just sat here in this meeting, feeling this energy come through me? Sometimes we are just called to sit and direct our focus in some particular direction, and it is up to us to obey. In this instance, I was energised and blessed.

So it has been that I have learnt the power of holding each other in the Light to facilitate healing, growth, and engaging in the world. The act of holding each other in the Light is a deliberate and intentional action that takes practice, focus, and energy and can effect a major transformation on others, their capacity for action, and what happens in the world.

It takes time and practice to build this skill and develop confidence in it. People new to Quakers are largely left to figure things out for themselves. A simple yet powerful activity for us as Quakers would be to regularly practice this holding of each other in the Light in pairs, taking turns and providing feedback to each other about the experience of holding and the experience of being held.

In undertaking such an exercise, it is important to have a sense of connecting to Spirit and being a part of something outside your direct control—the words "Thy will, not my will" come to mind. Steps that help with this include

- being grounded, centred, and relaxed in the body;

- calming the mind and, as holder, focusing on the other;

- coming from the heart and practicing holding the other without attachment to outcome; and

- having the gathering well held. Participants could take turns in holding the whole group and share how that experience was for them.

An important part of developing confidence in the development of this skill is providing feedback and sharing with each other what the experience of being held and holding was like.

How was the experience? (taking turns for the holder and holdee to speak)

What sensations were felt?

If there were lapses in concentration/focus, how did it feel to both the holdee and the holder?

Was it easy or difficult?

Was it similar or different to other times?

How much energy/effort did it take?

It is my hope that we will share in practical ways our knowledge and experience of holding an individual or group in the Light, especially with people new to Quakers. In doing so, we will be taking the time to deepen our spiritual practice, skills, and understanding as well as contributing something unique and powerful to meeting the current challenges of living in our world.

Source: Moira Darling, "Holding in the Light—My Experience," *The Australian Friend*, March 6, 2022, https://australianfriend.org/holding-in-the-light-my-experience/

Appendix 5

Eldering via Zoom

Jan Hoffman
Mt. Toby Friends Meeting, Leverett, Massachusetts

The Spring Must Be Opened

Dear Friends,

I want to tell you about one particular Zoom meeting for worship at Mt. Toby which stimulated me to engage with the query, "Is new experience teaching me the Spirit is present in places I have previously thought it couldn't be?"

If so, maybe I need to change. . . .[1]

For me, Zoom worship has been so liberating. In early February 2020 I had major surgery to reconstruct my hip after a fall. Confined to a hospital bed in our dining room, I couldn't attend worship at the meetinghouse. Then Covid came, and worship moved to Zoom on March 22. With what joy I saw faces of people in my spiritual ecosystem on my computer screen!

My experience of being gathered in a merciful, loving Presence was not shared by everyone, however. Many chose not to attend; others worshipped at home at the same time. Ministry and Worship (M&W) urged Friends to worship in varied ways, and one M&W member offered walking worship.

One Sunday, a chaotic spirit got into the Zoom worship. The first message was a scattering one; two messages immediately following tried unsuccessfully to draw the meeting back to center. The chaotic spirit was more than I could hold alone. "Where are other elders?" I cried internally. Many "messages" followed, some grounded, some not. Near the end of worship, a very centered message was offered, and the meeting closer invited us to "sink down to the Seed."

Instead, more speaking followed. At the end of my own capacity to pray, I remembered some words from Job Scott, an 18th-century Quaker: "[T]he spring must be opened in the hearer, or else there can be little profitable done by the speaker. [The speaker] must feel a door of entrance in the people's minds, or it is very difficult to get safely and relievingly forward."

Ah—ears must be opened! "Opening ears" is the work of elders in the body of the meeting. We too often limit our understanding of eldering to laboring with a speaker who has gone beyond their leading. We need elders who labor in the worship itself, preparing the soil for the seeds a speaker may sow or disciplining scattering spirits that may rise up.

After worship I got an email from the Friend who had spoken near the end of meeting. The message that had come through her started rising well before she was able to be faithful to it. It was a challenge to deal with technology in the process of finally offering her message, but she was grateful to have been able to do it. She was grateful for my presence; she spiritually held on to me, and felt me holding her. Could her email begin the conversation about her experience that wasn't possible after Zoom worship? These conversations are also part of an elder's work.

To M&W, I wrote: We need to feel more elders at work. When worship was in the meetinghouse, by 9:30 a.m. at least four of us would be seated in the four corners of the meeting room. Our sitting created a grounded space for worshippers to enter. Could I work on duplicating that in the context of Zoom? I asked M&W if it were possible for Friends to enter the Zoom worship room at 9:30, separating worshippers from those who needed technical help managing Zoom. Yes was the answer.

How could I engage elders? I realized that three of those "9:30 regulars" at the meetinghouse did not attend Zoom worship. I had carried a concern for elders at work in worship, and had experienced eldering from a distance.

I called one of the regulars to express my concern about that week's worship, and he responded: "Every Sunday I sit in my living room and hold Mt. Toby worship. I felt the chaos yesterday and wondered, 'What happened?' It was hard work holding it." I felt grateful for this elder's work. Another regular who worshipped at home asked me to name Friends who attended Zoom worship who I thought were elders and contact them. A third regular was holding the walking worship. All were comfortable with letting those in worship know these elders were holding the worship beginning at 9:30.

I called a regular Zoom worshipper who I felt had a gift for eldering. I told her what a difference it made to me to see her grounded presence on the Zoom screen each week—it helped me feel joined to others in the work. I asked if she might do that work more consciously, and she agreed.

The following Sunday I signed on to Zoom worship at 9:30 and was put in the worship room immediately. What a gift to be aware of those elders unseen on Zoom holding meeting with me, as well as the elder I had asked to come early to Zoom! The worship that week was centered and grounded, almost entirely silent. However, I knew that I was only one of the many folks on M&W and elsewhere who had prayed and acted according to their own discernment. This affirmed my faith that our worship can be nurtured by being aware of both ministers and elders at work as part of the living ecosystem of our meetings.

With immense gratitude for all I have learned among Friends,

Jan Hoffman, Mt Toby Meeting

Source: Jan Hoffman, "The Spring Must Be Opened," *New England Yearly Meeting of Friends (Quakers) Monthly Newsletter* (June 2021), https://mailchi.mp/neym/june-2021-the-spring-must-be-opened.

Appendix 6

Building Up the Life of Our Meetings: A Retreat for Those with a Call to Eldering and a Concern for Vital Worship— Eldering Consultation Report, January 2013

Planning Group for New York Yearly Meeting and
New England Yearly Meeting Eldering Consultation

We have people in our meetings whose way of being a Quaker is to ground and to hold an individual, a group, a meeting . . . to elder. In New England and New York we are learning this often silent ministry can lead an individual or the corporate body to new insights.

In December 2012, the first joint eldering consultation between New England and New York Yearly Meeting Friends was held at Woolman Hill Retreat Center in Deerfield, Massachusetts. The purpose of the retreat was to give Friends who have the gift of eldering an opportunity to share our experiences; to learn from one another; to explore the various ways in which we elder; to discuss the challenges we've face and how we deal with them; and to talk about how to draw out gifts of eldering in others.

A total of 42 people participated. The planning group developed lists of invitees from each yearly meeting. For New England, 21 Friends were invited, of whom 20 registered and 19 attended (one registrant had to cancel due to a loved one's death). For New York, 26 Friends were invited, of whom 15 attended.

Five members of the planning group attended: three from New England Yearly Meeting, two from New York Yearly Meeting (an additional member of that yearly meeting was not able to attend due to scheduling conflicts). Woolman Hill staff member Margaret Cooley also participated in the

188

planning group and in the retreat itself. Ken and Katharine Jacobsen (Ohio Yearly Meeting [Conservative]) served as the facilitation team.

There was an incredibly strong response to the invitation, and we decided to accept everyone who registered rather than limit the number who could participate. That meant that we housed seven people at a nearby motel to ease overcrowding in the Woolman Hill overnight accommodations. This arrangement seemed to work well. The group size was larger than we'd initially planned for, and for future gatherings we recommend either adding members to the facilitation team or decreasing the number of participants. Throughout the planning, we were aware that the list of those invited was in no way comprehensive, that there are many Friends with eldering gifts in our midst, and that this gathering would be only a first step.

Strengths of the gathering included the diversity of age, the breadth of meetings represented, and intentionally drawing participants from more than one yearly meeting. We were blessed by the rich tradition and knowledge of eldering in the Conservative branch brought by Ken and Katharine. Despite the diversity of styles, perspectives, and reactions, we were struck by a palpable commonality and by a deep hunger to connect around experiences of eldering. The dialogue between New England and New York Friends was particularly fruitful, and many participants expressed hope that it will continue.

During our opening night, we were asked this query: "To me, at this time, the primary work of the elder is _______________." These were just three of the responses.

- To listen to the breath of truth breathing through the collective body

- To mind the center and to aid in its revelation

- To be centered in the Presence, in God, and from that center to anchor the individual or group for whom he or she is being elder

The complete list of responses is at the end of this report.

Those of us on the planning team looked at this consultation as somewhat of an experiment. We had a tentative plan, but while waiting on Spirit, vocal ministry led us to a different place. We made space for a concern and for what followed that concern. The body prayer that Ken and Katharine Jacobsen shared with us, and which was repeated a number of times throughout the weekend, grounded us: "release and return, encounter and accept, attend and live out." Throughout, we were graced by the eldership of Ken and Katharine.

These were just some of the responses to "What has been most helpful to you in this workshop? What learnings will you take away?"

- The gathered witness and acknowledgment that eldering is one of the Gifts of the Spirit

- Communion with other Friends and with God. The keen awareness of Ken and Katharine in following Spirit and their willingness to release expectation and normal time conventions in order to be honest and Truthful to God was perhaps the best example for us all and with which I will walk away

- Sharing with others; learning that we have much to help each other with

- That we are all varied in condition and experience and the overall learning is to welcome this and to be at peace with it—it is all just a blink of God's eye

This consultation was a beginning. Next steps might include planning a weekend that would focus on concrete tips for carrying out the work of eldering (Eldering 101), providing opportunities for Friends to share the actual joys and challenges of eldering within and beyond our meetings, gatherings of elders on a quarterly or regional level, and scheduling annual gatherings of New York/New England elders.

In our closing worship, a Friend offered the following quote: "We have not succeeded in answering all our problems. The answers we have found only serve to raise a whole set of new questions. In some ways we feel we are as confused as ever but we believe we are confused on a higher level and about more important things."[1]

Planning Group

New York Yearly Meeting: Lu Harper, Kristina Keefe-Perry, Anne Pomeroy

New England Yearly Meeting: Margaret Cooley, Ann Dodd-Collins, Kristna Evans, Janet Gibian Hough

Responses to Query

The primary work of the elder is:

- To hold the container for the body

- To be a servant of God

- To support, to listen

- To always show up, be a consistent presence reflecting the light and love within the community in service to truth

- To lead by being a living example of the transformative power of love and of humility

- To nurture individuals and the body in living ever more fully into faithfulness to the call of truth and Love

- To ground every encounter in/with integrity

- To be with those who minister—to listen, to be in constant prayer, to walk beside, to reflect back

- Grounding the group or individual, rooting to the Spirit

- To listen to the breath of truth breathing through the collective body

- To watch what comes/unfolds

- To love, hold in love

- To provide guidance to those in pain, those grieving, and going through hardship, but not to forget their own pain. An elder is kind of like a wise therapist that won't charge you money.

- To behold another as God beholds that person—with love, love, love—tender regard and clarity

- To be used by God in creating space for encounters with the Holy—in individuals and in groups. To be used by God in God's ministry to us as the Body of Christ.

- To strengthen—through prayer, presence, holding in the Light—individuals in whom the Spirit is moving, the meeting as a whole, situations, questions alive in the meeting arising to more deeply call forth the Spirit within it

- To bring/feel/recognize God's presence and love and to hold others in it

- To hold my pastor in a loving space, and to hold my meeting in a loving space—Light-filled, gentle, enveloping, and loving space

- To be midwife to ministry—accompany, comfort, watch the health of minister and message

- To hold the space, to hold the center, to channel love/energy, to reflect love/energy, to deflect other

- To mind the center and to aid in its revelation

- Holding a Holy Space—finding it, embracing it, in Love

- To lovingly hold and nurture the person or community that is seeking to do God's will

- To listen to God within self, group, other individuals and reflect that as needed

- To hold the meeting in prayer

- To hold up the veil we imagine separates us from God, that we might see past it. To listen always for love

- To nurture and to guide; to be open and to love selflessly and self-fully

- To listen deeply; to love deeply; to be ever vigilant; to empty oneself of one's self, so that the Divine Presence flows freely within and without; being examples of love, light, truth, and compassion

- To love and to radically trust that the Divine Teacher intends to use you to draw love into the world and out of those around you and make it more visible

- Encouraging nurturer

- To midwife God's reality into the present through creating a space, holding the vision, and embodying the hope of the body she/he serves

- To bear witness to God's presence and to abide with those who suffer

- To love and to name and nurture gifts of the Spirit in others

- To encourage and facilitate growth

- To dissolve self into receptive prayer for, and discernment in, the Body—the living embodiment of Spirit

- To hold and lift up before God the gathered body and/or individuals within the body

- To be centered in the Presence, in God, and from that center to anchor the individual or group for whom he or she is being elder

- To listen; to spiritually discern, to seek guidance from the Holy Spirit

- To love the meeting; this action will happen in a variety of ways, through prayer, listening, being present, writing, teaching. At its basis, the command, gift and blessed work is simply and completely to love the meeting.

- To channel God's love fully into the present moment

Source: Planning Group for New York Yearly Meeting and New England Yearly Meeting Eldering Consultation, "Building Up the

Life of Our Meetings: A Retreat for Those with a Call to Eldering and a Concern for Vital Worship—Eldering Consultation Report," January 2013. The text has been slightly edited.

Appendix 7

The Course Elder's Role at Silver Wattle Quaker Centre

Silver Wattle Quaker Centre

Online eldering

You may be invited to serve as an Elder for an online course at Silver Wattle. While there are many similarities in fulfilling this role whether in a residential or online environment, there are some differences which we highlight in this section.

Unlike a residential course or event, online courses may include blocks of time online or shorter periods of time online over several weeks.

Discerning if this spiritual work is for you to do at this time

- How comfortable are you with the technical side of Zoom or similar platforms? While another Friend will serve as Zoom host and technical support, the Elder is still expected to be present and visible throughout the sessions.

- How stable is your internet connection? Do you have access to a laptop, desktop or tablet and a suitable space?

- Even though you won't be physically traveling to serve as Elder for the course, it is a physical, emotional and spiritual commitment.

- Unlike residential courses, you'll still be living with flatmates/family members/pets. Are they reasonably understanding that you will be occupied online during the course?

- Just like during a residential course, you and the facilitator will have regular check-in times, and participants may also want to speak with you. The difference, of course, is that such conversations can't take place in person or over a cuppa. How comfortable are you talking over the phone or via Facetime/Zoom?

- Discuss with your presenter the relevance of your availability between sessions.

Before the course:

- Make sure you have a support person. Talk with the Elders' Committee if someone is not assigned to you when you are appointed to elder the specific course.

- Making contact with the course facilitator is as important as in the lead-up to a residential course.

- Arrange for regular times to talk with the facilitator during the course, checking to see how they are traveling.

- It's likely that there will also one or more meetings with the facilitator and the tech team—it's important for the Elder to also attend these meetings. You'll be holding not only the facilitator, but also the tech team throughout the course, and the preparation sessions are part of this process. It's important that everyone knows what is expected of them.

- Talk with the tech team about arranging a break-out room to serve as the Elder's Room where you can talk privately with individuals as needed.

- Talk with the facilitator and the tech team about socializing opportunities (e.g. morning tea on line).

- Talk with the course facilitator about introducing you at the start of the course and explain your role and how participants can contact you during the course—both during and after course hours (as agreed to with presenter).

- Undertake your own spiritual preparations just as you would if you were eldering a residential event or course.

- Consider the space you'll use as Elder during the course. Is it a place where distractions are limited and where others in the household won't distract you (at least too much)?

During the course:

- Rename your screen name to include 'Elder' and a contact detail (e.g. Margaret Fell, Elder, m 040123445).

- Specify the times you would be available as Elder between sessions (after your discussion with the presenter/facilitator).

- Ensure that participants are aware of your role and that it's okay to contact you. Let them know when you plan to rest and recharge daily (e.g. 'My silent time is 1–1:30 during the afternoon break time').

- Let participants know that if they don't complete the course, you as Elder will be in touch to see how they are going.

- Make time to rest and recharge before and after sessions.

- Don't let the technology distract you—it's vital to listen carefully and to follow the Spirit's leading.

- Keep in mind that unlike a residential experience, the online world makes it harder to pick up on physical/visual cues, especially without the informal opportunities of shared meals and spaces.

- Be available to talk with the facilitator and/or course participants via phone or Facetime during meal times and other breaks throughout the course.

- Check in with your support person, even if everything is fine.

After the course:

- Immediately following the course is usually a good time for a short debriefing with both the facilitator and the tech team. This could be followed by a more in-depth discussion with the facilitator.

- Touch base or debrief with your support person.

Source: Silver Wattle Quaker Centre, "The Course Elder's Role at Silver Wattle Quaker Centre." Unpublished, n.d. Published here in slightly edited form. For a full copy of the Silver Wattle guidelines, contact the Silver Wattle office at admin.office@silverwattle.org.au.

Appendix 8

Nurturing Ministers: Isaac Alexander
Predicts a Great Mortality

Brian Drayton
Souhegan Friends Meeting, Milford, New Hampshire

This case study is drawn from the Journal of Samuel Bownas. Early in his ministry, which began around 1696, Samuel Bownas developed a strong sense of kinship with Isaac Alexander (1680–1705), who "appeared in the ministry" about the same time as Bownas did. Bownas's journal portrays them learning about their work in the ministry, and comparing notes with each other.

In Bownas's account, early in their ministry, Isaac goes to Bristol "yearly meeting" (a regional meeting for worship held annually), and finds himself led to offer challenging ministry. He forthrightly accused Friends of slackness and unfaithfulness. This message in itself might have been unsettling or irritating, but would not have been unusual, though Friends since the Toleration act (1689) had responded to the end of most persecution by building lives and doing business, and the militancy of prior years faded. Isaac, however, felt led to predict that continued unfaithfulness would bring on calamity, and Bristol Friends were taken aback.

> Isaac [Alexander] went to Bristol yearly meeting, and was very zealous against unnecessary fashions and superfluities in both sexes; insomuch, that some thought he did, in his words against them, exceed the bounds of modesty: the chief objection was, concerning his prophesying of a great mortality, which the Lord was about to bring as a judgment upon the people, for their pride and wickedness; which he thought it his duty to deliver in their yearly-meeting,

as a warning for all to mind their ways, lest being taken unprepared, their loss should be irreparable: which he did in such strong and positive terms, that Friends were afraid he was too much exalted in himself . . .

The intensity and certitude with which Isaac spoke moved some elders to wonder about the source of the message, and so they undertook to explore the question with Isaac. Note that they came to him with an attitude of caution, but also of inquiry. What would that conversation have been like? I imagine that there would have been a spoken and an unspoken element.

Aloud, they would be asking him questions about the message itself but even more about how he felt before, during, and after the message. Was there a moment during the preaching when he felt himself pushing beyond what was given to him? Did he feel any uneasiness when this material arose? Was he feeling anger, or disdain, or some other judgmental condition, or did he feel truly that he was remaining in the cool stream of divine love which should be present at the heart of a message? When he sat down, did he feel the reward of peace, or did he rather feel some sense of discomfort or rebuke?

The unspoken part of the conversation would be a careful feeling after the young man's condition, noting whether his answers to them were defensive or self-assertive. They would probably have felt, as Luke Howard wrote about Job Scott, that a minister, especially a young one, might sometimes be expected to show:

> a perceptible excess on the side of the imagination and the feelings [as] had been the case with many good and useful men before him: and such a temperament makes a minister faithful, or courageous and energetic in the discharge of duty, but in measure disqualifies him from being a competent judge of doctrine and controversies.

Thus, they may well have felt that Isaac was on the whole a promising young minister, in need not of suppression, but of guidance towards a better understanding, and thus usefulness in the important work of the ministry. They reached clarity that he was not at that time in a safe condition, and that he had wandered from the leading which brought him to Bristol. Accordingly, they sent him home, no doubt annotating his travel minute or otherwise communicating with the ministers and elders there about their sense of this painful event:

> some of the elders thought proper to converse with, and examine him concerning this extraordinary message which he had delivered; but what he said to them not being satisfactory, they advised him to proceed no farther on his journey, but to return home; which he did under great trouble . . .

When he got home, interestingly, Isaac was not in the dog house. Having returned to the meeting that had care of him, and that had recognized his gift, he took up his life and work as before.

> he was there received in much love and tenderness, and appeared in his gift very excellent, and grew in Divine wisdom and power, being of great service in the ministry wherever he came.

This was a time when the meetings of ministers (increasingly augmented by the addition of elders) would engage in explicit conversations about the ministry offered in the meeting, based on a spirit of watchfulness for the presence of "life" in what was offered. This, I think, should be inferred in the background from the next episode in the story. Isaac once again felt a leading to travel in the ministry. He spoke to some of the meeting's elders. They cautioned him not to go—not categorically, but not until they could consult with Friends in Bristol. They examined Isaac again, and heard how the earlier event felt to him in retrospect, and then wrote to Bristol:

> And he having a concern to visit the churches abroad, and acquainting some of our elders therewith, they thought it not proper for him to go, till something was done to satisfy the Friends of Bristol; and upon their enquiry of Isaac, he gave them a single and honest account how it was with him at that time, respecting his concern: so Friends took it in hand, and wrote to

Bristol, neither justifying nor condemning him, but recommended charity and tenderness towards him.

They would not have "recommended charity and tenderness" if their experience of him in the meeting since his return from Bristol had caused any uneasiness in their minds. The Bristol Friends returned a message

> that with open arms they could receive him, believing him to be a sincere young man, who intended very well; and they were glad he took their admonition right, and had owned it had been of service to him.

Bownas's summary of the event is interesting. Isaac, in retrospect at the time, did not think that he had mistaken his leading, at least not in the sense of putting too much of self or misplaced zeal into the warnings he uttered. Yet he nevertheless felt that Bristol Friends had treated him appropriately; he felt he had been treated well, and trusted their discernment. In the event, he was settled more firmly in his gift and service.

> Thus ended this affair, and Isaac said he could not think hard of his brethren in doing what he did, though he could not then see that he had missed his way, in delivering that prophecy: thus shewing forth a lively instance of a warm zeal, tempered with a due regard to the sense and advice of his brethren and elders, and the unity of the church, which doubtless tended to his comfort and preservation.

I will note here a few points of interest in conclusion:

- Isaac was exercising his gift as openly, and we might say passionately, as he could—perhaps pushing boundaries to explore the extent of his capacities at this time.

- He was not surprised that the elders of the meeting he was visiting exercised oversight of his ministry. The brief account suggests that they were not censorious, but when something made them uneasy, they felt it their place to inquire more attentively.

- A point to note here is that in the "apostolic era" of Quakerism, public Friends were considered to be as members of the meetings they visited. This notion continued into the era of separations later, and alas was abused in the midst of controversy. In our case, however, Isaac did not object that the elders of Bristol would have the same care of him as would those in his home meeting, and the Bristol elders exercised their responsibility. Their caution suggested some understanding that a visiting minister might bring messages, or speak in a manner, to which they were unaccustomed (and in a way that is part of the "point" or benefit of such visits, when done in the Spirit).

- The "elders" at this time (around 1700) would not necessarily have been "elders" in the sense we know it (that is, occupying a specific, identified office). It is likely that the term still had the connotation of someone "well grown in the truth."

- Isaac maintained a sense of freedom to follow his calling—there is no sense from the account that he came home and kept silent. He carried on with a ministry that was not abrogated by one possible mistake—but I think that if he had responded to the Bristol elders with disrespect, or if he had returned and spoken in anger or defensiveness, the meeting would have seriously questioned whether in that condition he could rightly discern his way.

Source: Brian Drayton, "Nurturing Ministers: Isaac Alexander Predicts a Great Mortality." *Amor Vincat*, December 28, 2018. www.amorvincat.wordpress.com/2018/12/. Published here in slightly edited form with permission from Brian Drayton.

Appendix 9

The Challenges of Accompanying Ministers in Their Humanity

Elaine Emily

Strawberry Creek Friends Meeting, Berkeley, California

A long time ago, I made a list of all the pieces of ministry I had accompanied and the ministers that had carried them.[1] There were well over a hundred names of ministers. Some accompaniment was in person. Some lasted for an hour or so. Some took place from a distance rather than in person. And many involved my physically traveling with the minister for a week or more.

A number of the folks I have traveled with have been sexually abused or otherwise traumatized as children. Often, trauma causes an opening for Spirit to enter more fully. While this may not always lead the person into a public ministry, it is often the case for many of our Quaker ministers.

Because of my clinical training in psychotherapy, I recognize when a minister is disassociating, either while delivering deep ministry or at other times. Often, the minister struggles with Spirit to be faithful to a piece of hard ministry they have been given to deliver. Some yell and scream, some throw things, some just retreat—some into a little ball. One person wrote page after page, none of which was ever used, although I have no doubt it was an important part of their preparation.

One trip I particularly remember lasted two and a half weeks, and we spent almost every minute together—even sharing the same bedroom wherever we went. The minister wanted me to be at their side at all times. There were some really lovely moments with just the two of us. We did ceremony, prayed together, and shared life stories. It was clear to me that there were mental health issues, and I would have loved some accompaniment myself, someone to help me figure out how to move forward faithfully with the least harm to all involved. Despite this minister's large gifts of ministry, they were isolated because of mental health issues and other circumstances, and their neediness in turn isolated me. Under different circumstances, I would have had plenty of opportunities to connect deeply and replenish my own well. But in this particular instance, that was not the case. Plus, it felt like I needed to keep my experience secret, even from other elders.

Now, I have a group of identified elders that I feel not only free to share with but obligated to be transparent with about my experiences. Of course, I don't share tender pieces of a minister's life willy-nilly, but I also don't keep secrets about folks' behavior that doesn't align with Spirit. It becomes a tricky bind when a minister uses alcohol or other drugs that get in the way of their spiritual groundedness. When do I keep traveling with them in ministry? And when and how do I intervene, or should I not intervene at all? I need to trust my Inner Guide, especially if there isn't a way to check or test with others.

The same goes for sexual encounters because spiritual authority and power are very attractive. I know people of both sexes who have inappropriately offered themselves sexually to ministers and then felt hurt and disruptive to the community when they were correctly rejected. On the other hand, I've also known ministers who were sexually inappropriate. Again, when and how should I intervene on the behalf of an individual or the community?

The same dilemma goes for violence, domestic or otherwise, including bullying. What about engagement with pornography? Misogyny? Racism? Homophobia? Able-ism? Misuse of money? These are all human issues, and elders see them show up in the ministers they travel with when they allow themselves to see and know.

How to proceed is not always crystal clear to me. Naming the troubling behavior out loud to the minister is a first step. Sometimes, bringing the issue to a larger group is important. More than one person has asked me how I can continue to accompany various powerful ministers with troubling behavior; they feel I should not be lending my spiritual power and accompaniment to them.

I pray. I go to my accountability committee appointed by my meeting. I confer with other trusted elders. I only accompany folks I feel God has put on my "plate." I do not think they are perfect; I am very aware that part of my concern is for the wider community's safety and integrity.

In my yearly meeting, there was a very revered man who gave sage spiritual advice to many as a spiritual director and as an elder accompanying ministry. It was later discovered that he was a pedophile and had abused his own children many years before. Many of us struggled to make sense of these two realities that were revealed to us. Was he good? Was he bad? Could we trust the guidance we had come to rely on from him? To me, this is a spiritual paradox we all live with every day. The best of us and the worst of us reside inside each of us. Early Friends spoke about the seed of Christ and the seed of the serpent—the two seeds. Both need to be brought into the light, into consciousness, and to our faith community.

We as elders need to make sure we don't enable bad behavior and that we encourage Friends to walk more fully in the Light. People can and do change.

Writing all of this stirs up visceral feelings in me from each of these memory experiences. Of course, now, twenty or thirty years later, I might do things very differently. The memories do not elicit shame or blame, rather just recognition of the struggle to be faithful in unknown, new territory. Early on, one of my spiritual disciplines was to live my life as transparently as possible. What if whatever I did was on the front page of the local newspaper? Could I live with myself with my head held high? Even though I saw and knew things that were uncomfortable and sometimes painful to me, I think I was able to mostly focus on the ministry rather than on me or the person I was accompanying.

A couple of times I have had to say, "This needs to change, right now, or I'm leaving." Once I said it for the safety of the community, and once I said it because the minister was going beyond the Light they had been given. These are hard and uncomfortable experiences, and when they happen it is very hard to stay committed to Spirit, love, and concern for the minister and the community and to love and have compassion for myself. In situations like these, it would be a great gift to have another elder to consult with and accompany myself and the minister. I can't imagine what it would look or feel like if I had to leave or if I was "fired" as an elder during a time of ministry.

I share these things because, as elders, we often see beneath the surface. We often see ugly truths that others don't see or don't want to see. Also, as a group, Quakers are hesitant to talk about uncomfortable truths. Elders need to discern boldly how to proceed when encountering difficult truths.

Bibliography

Australia Yearly Meeting of the Religious Society of Friends (Quakers). *This We Can Say: Australian Quaker Life, Faith and Thought*. Queensland: Australia Yearly Meeting of the Religious Society of Friends (Quakers), 2008.

Barnett, Craig. "Spiritual Eldership." *Transition Quaker* (blog). April 8, 2016. https://transitionquaker.blogspot.com/2016/04/spiritual-eldership.html.

Boulding, Elise. *One Small Plot of Heaven: Reflections on Family Life by a Quaker Sociologist*. Wallingford PA: Pendle Hill Publications, 1989.

Bownas, Samuel. *A Description of the Qualifications Necessary to a Gospel Minister*. Philadelphia: Pendle Hill Publications and Tract Association of Friends, 1989. First published 1750 by The Bible in George-Yard (London).

Braithwaite, William Charles. *Spiritual Guidance in the Experience of the Society of Friends*. 1909 Swarthmore Lecture. London: Headley Brothers, 1909. https://archive.org/details/cu31924084550098.

Brown, Michael. "The Right Way to Disagree with Spiritual Elders." *Voices* (blog). *Christian Post*, September 3, 2019. www.christianpost.com/voices/the-right-way-to-disagree-with-spiritual-elders.html.

Cadbury, Henry. "My Personal Religion." *Universalist Friends* 35 (Fall/Winter 2000). https://nyym.org/content/thoughts-eldering.

Cadbury, Mary Foster. "Thoughts on Eldering." *Spark* (New York Yearly Meeting), 51, no. 3 (May 2021). www.nyym.org/content/spark-may-2021-eldership-and-spiritual-accompaniment.

Cronk, Sandra. *Gospel Order: A Quaker Understanding of Faithful Church Community*. Pendle Hill Pamphlet #297. Wallingford, PA: Pendle Hill Publications, 1991.

Darling, Moira. "Holding in the Light—My Experience." *The Australian Friend*, March 6, 2022, https://australianfriend.org/holding-in-the-light-my-experience/.

Drayton, Brian. "Nurturing Ministers: Isaac Alexander Predicts a Great Mortality." *Amor Vincat*, December 28, 2018. www.amorvincat.wordpress.com/2018/12/.

Drayton, Brian. *On Living with a Concern for Gospel Ministry*. Revised edition. Philadelphia: Quaker Press of Friends General Conference, 2006.

Emily, Elaine. *The Quaker Practice of Traveling with an Elder*. Video interview by Jon Watts. *QuakerSpeak*. Uploaded November 15, 2018. www.youtube.com/watch?v=kP4Ry27ZJmY.

Emily, Elaine, Bob Schmitt, Cathy Walling, Gordon Bishop, and Mary Kay Glazer. *Reflections by Five Quaker Elders*. Unpublished 2006 audio recording and transcript. In Elaine Emily's possession.

Fell, Margaret. "An Epistle to Convinced but not yet Crucified Friends, in 1656." In Margaret Fell, *A Brief Collection of Remarkable Passages*, London, 1710 (106–14). http://dqc.esr.earlham.edu:8080/xmlmm/loginB?XMLMMToc =E3109149&XMLMMLanguage=English&XMLMMCollection= /earlham&XMLMMReturnURL=http://esr.earlham.edu/dqc/bi blio.html.

Ferris, David. *Resistance and Obedience to God: Memoirs of David Ferris (1707–1779)*. Edited by Martha Paxson Grundy. Philadelphia: Friends General Conference, 2001.

Fitz-Hugh, Lynn. "Friends and Conflict." *The Friendly Seeker* (blog). October 30, 2019. http://thefriendlyseeker.blogspot.com/ 2019/10/it-may-not-surprise-you-to-hear-me-say_30.html.

Gates, Thomas. *Members One of Another: The Dynamics of Membership in Quaker Meeting*. Pendle Hill Pamphlet #371. Wallingford, PA: Pendle Hill Publications, 2004.

Harper, Lu. "Introduction to Eldership and Spiritual Accompaniment." *Spark* (New York Yearly Meeting), 51, no. 3 (May 2021). https://nyym.org/content/introduction-eldership-and-spiritual-accompaniment.

Harper, Lu, and Kenn Harper. "Nurturing the Spiritual Life of the Meeting." Unpublished paper, November 2007.

Henderson, Dorothy, and Gordon Bishop. "To Elder: The Verb Reclaimed." Unpublished paper, 2021.

Hoffman, Jan. "The Spring Must Be Opened." *New England Yearly Meeting of Friends (Quakers) Monthly Newsletter* (June 2021). https://mailchi.mp/neym/june-2021-the-spring-must-be-opened.

Hole, Francis D., and Ellie Shacter. *A Little Journal of Devotions out of Quaker Worship: An Experiment with 104 Entries across Two Thousand Miles*. Philadelphia: Quaker Press of FGC, 2001.

Jacobsen, Katharine. "Eldering as a Spiritual Gift." *Conservative Friend* (Eighth Month 2007). https://inwardlight.org/faith/eldership/eldering-spiritual-gift.

Keefe-Perry, Kristina. "Tentmaker, Tailor: Friends as Bivocational Ministers." Panel presentation at the Quaker Theological Discussion Group, December 12, 2020. YouTube video, 50:00 to 1:13:04. https://www.youtube.com/watch?v=qb7IoZH8jos&t=3959s.

Kelly, Beth. "Holding Space." *Spark* (New York Yearly Meeting) 51, no. 3 (May 2021). www.nyym.org/content/spark-may-2021-eldership-and-spiritual-accompaniment.

Kimmerer, Robin Wall. *Braiding Sweetgrass: Indigenous Wisdom, Scientific Knowledge, and the Teachings of Plants*. Minneapolis: Milkweed Editions, 2013.

Lape, Herb. "A Case for Eldering and Discipline." *Friends Journal* 55, no. 4 (April 2009): 10–11.

Larrabee, Margery Mears. *Spirit-Led Eldering: Integral to Our Faith and Practice*. Pendle Hill Pamphlet #392. Wallingford, PA: Pendle Hill Publications, 2007.

Loring, Patricia. *Listening Spirituality Vol. II: Corporate Spiritual Practice among Friends*. Washington Grove, MD: Openings Press, 1999.

New England Yearly Meeting. *Interim Faith and Practice 2014 (2015 Edition*. Worcester, MA: New England Yearly Meeting of Friends. https://neym.org/read-approved-chapters-faith-and-practice.

North Carolina Yearly Meeting (Conservative). *Faith and Practice: Book of Discipline of the North Carolina Yearly Meeting (Conservative) of the Religious Society of Friends*. North Carolina: North Carolina Yearly Meeting (Conservative), 1983.

Nouwen, Henri. "Yearning for Perfect Love." Henri Nouwen Society, January 20, 2018. https://henrinouwen.org/meditations/yearning-perfect-love/.

O'Reilley, Mary Rose. "Deep Listening." *Friends Journal* 40, no. 11 (November 1994): 16–18.

O'Reilley, Mary Rose. *Radical Presence: Teaching as Contemplative Practice*. Portsmouth, NH: Heinemann Educational Books, 1998.

Pacific Yearly Meeting. "Epistle from the 75th Annual Session of Pacific Yearly Meeting of the Religious Society of Friends, 2021. https://www.pacificyearlymeeting.org/wordpress/wp-content/uploads/2021/08/Pacific-YM-2021-Epistle.pdf.

Pacific Yearly Meeting. *Faith and Practice: A Guide to Quaker Discipline in the Experience of Pacific Yearly Meeting of the Religious Society of Friends*. San Francisco: Pacific Yearly Meeting, 1985.

Pacific Yearly Meeting. *Faith and Practice: A Guide to Quaker Discipline in the Experience of Pacific Yearly Meeting of the Religious Society of Friends*. Pacific Yearly Meeting, 2001.

Penington, Isaac. "Some Directions to the Panting Soul." In *The Works of the Long-mournful and Sorely-distressed Isaac Penington* . . . (pp. 482–89). London: S. Clark, 1761. https://www.google.com/books/edition/The_Works_of_the_L ong_mournful_and_Sorel/yoRjNtPg_DwC?hl=en&gbpv=0.

Philadelphia Yearly Meeting Spiritual Formation Collaborative. "Elders and Eldering." Philadelphia Yearly Meeting of the Religious Society of Friends, October 2009. https://www.pym.org/spiritual-formation-program-collaborative/for-facilitators/organizing-issues/elders-and-eldering/.

Planning Group for New York Yearly Meeting and New England Yearly Meeting Eldering Consultation. "Building Up the Life of Our Meetings: A Retreat for Those with a Call to Eldering and a Concern for Vital Worship—Eldering Consultation Report." January 2013.

Pomeroy, Anne. "Letting Go of the Term 'Elder.'" *Spark* (New York Yearly Meeting) 51, no. 3 (May 2021). https://nyym.org/content/letting-go-term-elder.

Ramos, Angel. "The Gift of Traveling with Each Other." *Spark* (New York Yearly Meeting) 51, no. 3 (May 2021). https://nyym.org/content/gift-traveling-each-other

Reixach, Karen. "Recording as a Form of Eldering." *Spark* (New York Yearly Meeting) 51, no. 3 (May 2021). https://nyym.org/content/recording-form-eldering.

Rosales, Luis. "De noche iremos." Words by Luis Rosales with music by Jacques Berthier for the Taizé Community. Taizé , France: Les Presses de Taizé, 1986.

Routh, Martha Winter. *Memoir of the Life, Travels, and Religious Experience, of Martha Routh.* London: W. Alexander, 1822. https://www.google.com/books/edition/Memoir_of_the_Life_ Travels_and_Religious/xOleAAAAcAAJ?hl=en&gbpv=1.

Routledge, Jenny. *Living Eldership: A Journey of Discovery.* London: Quaker Books, 2014.

Rustin, Bayard. "In Apprehension How Like a God!" 1948 William Penn Lecture. Philadelphia: 1948. https://quaker.org/ legacy/pamphlets/wpl1948a.html.

Sánchez-Eppler, Benigno. "Bible Half Hour with Sánchez-Eppler." FGC Virtual Gathering 2021, YouTube, June 29, 2021. https://www.youtube.com/watch?v=5u9pWH8AavY.

Silver Wattle Quaker Centre. "The Course Elder's Role at Silver Wattle Quaker Centre." Unpublished, n.d.

Smith, Susan. "Overview: Eldering as Encouragement to Faithfulness." In *So That You Come Behind in No Gift: Ohio Yearly Meeting's Gathering on Eldering 6/20–22/1996*, 1–2. Barnesville, OH: Ohio Yearly Meeting (Conservative).

Steere, Douglas V. *On Listening to Another.* New York: Harper & Brothers, 1955.

Taber, William. "Contemporary Examples of Eldering—Panel: Marilyn Neyer, Nancy Hawkins, William Taber." In *So That You Come Behind in No Gift, Ohio Yearly Meeting's Gathering on Eldering 6/20–22/1996, 18–20.* Barnesville, OH: Ohio Yearly Meeting (Conservative).

Taber, William. *The Prophetic Stream*. Pendle Hill Pamphlet #256. Wallingford, PA: Pendle Hill Publications, 1984.

Taber, William P. Jr. "Introduction." In *A Description of the Qualifications Necessary to a Gospel Minister: Advice to Ministers and Elders Among the People Called Quakers by Samuel Bownas (1676–1753)*. Philadelphia: Pendle Hill Publications and Tract Association of Friends, 1989. First published 1750 by The Bible in George-Yard (London).

Tarter, Michelle Lise. "'Go North!' The Journey towards First-Generation Friends and Their Prophecy of Celestial Flesh." In *The Creation of Quaker Theory: Insider Perspectives*, edited by Pink Dandelion, 83–98. Aldershot, Hants, England: Routledge, 2004.

Ulanov, Ann, and Barry Ulanov. *Cinderella and Her Sisters: The Envied and the Envying*. Philadelphia: Westminster Press, 1983.

Walling, Cathy, and Elaine Emily. *Spiritual Accompaniment: An Experience of Two Friends Traveling in the Ministry*. Pendle Hill Pamphlet #428. Wallingford, PA: Pendle Hill Publications, 2014.

Wilson, Lloyd Lee. *Essays on the Quaker Vision of Gospel Order*. Philadelphia, PA: Quaker Press of Friends General Conference, 2007.

Wilson, Lloyd Lee. *Memoir of the Life and Religious Labors of Lloyd Lee Wilson, a Minister of the Gospel of the Religious Society of Friends, Particularly of North Carolina Yearly Meeting (Conservative)*. San Francisco: Inner Light Books, 2021.

Woolman, John. *The Journal of John Woolman*. Volume 1, part 2. The Harvard Classics. New York: P. F. Collier & Son, 1909–1914. https://www.bartleby.com/1/2/8.html.

Notes

Chapter 1: An Invitation

[1] Jacobsen, "Eldering as a Spiritual Gift."

[2] Harper, "Introduction to Eldership and Spiritual Accompaniment," 1, 4.

[3] Wilson, *Memoir*, 235.

[4] Larrabee, *Spirit-Led Eldering*, 3–4.

[5] Joseph Garren, personal communication. Hereafter, all reflections, interludes, and appendices that do not have a source cited in an endnote are from personal communications to the authors of this book between 2018 and 2022.

Interlude 1: To Elder: The Verb Reclaimed

[1] Pacific Yearly Meeting, *Faith and Practice: A Guide to Quaker Discipline in the Experience of Pacific Yearly Meeting of the Religious Society of Friends*, 1985. The 2001 revision of the Pacific Yearly Meeting *Faith and Practice* gives the following definition:

> *elder*—(1) *verb*, to support and encourage members or attenders in the flowering of spirit-led *ministry* (and discourage behavior and speech which inhibits ministry). This leadership can include logistical support, honest feedback, prayer, and helping with spiritual discernment. (2) *noun*, sometimes used to refer to one who has been chosen to provide ongoing eldering to support the ministry of one Friend. Historically, elders were appointed to foster the life of the meeting and individuals in the meeting.

[2] Henderson and Bishop, "To Elder."

Chapter 2: Gardens, Forests, and Fungi

[1] Routh, *Memoir*, 239. We are grateful to Brian Drayton for bringing Martha Routh's diary to our attention through his blog post "Speaking about Life in the Spirit 6: Not Just Metaphor," *Amor Vincat*, February 14, 2021, https://amorvincat.wordpress.com/2021/02/14/speaking-about-life-in-the-spirit-6-not-just-metaphors/.

[2] This section was partly inspired by Bob Schmitt's talk "Hope in Reflected Light," the first of three talks in a series in September and October 2020, in which Bob tells the story of his creative process of painting "Dawn at Mather Point, Grand Canyon" during the age of Covid-19. See Bob Schmitt, "Week One: Hope in Reflected Light" (video), Laughing Waters Studio, https://www.shopatlaughingwatersstudio.com/theartofhope. The authors thank Bob Schmitt for his insight into gardening as a metaphor.

[3] Mica Estrada, personal communication.

4 Carolyn Metzler, "Wilderness Spirituality" retreat description, https://www.carolynmetzler.com/retreats-and-workshops.

5 Braithwaite, *Spiritual Guidance*, 65–67. We are grateful to Lu and Kenn Harper for directing us to this source.

6 Carolyn Metzler, personal communication with Mary Kay Glazer. The authors thank Carolyn for her insight into wilderness as a metaphor.

7 Rosales, "De noche iremos."

8 Kimmerer, *Braiding Sweetgrass*, 20.

9 Carl Magruder, personal communication with Elaine Emily.

10 Carl Magruder, personal communication with the authors.

11 "Cultivate (v)" and "Forest (n)," *Online Etymology Dictionary*, www.etymonline.com/search?q=cultivate and www.etymonline.com/search?q=forest.

Chapter 3: Qualities of an Elder

1 This often-quoted phrase is from the journal of early Quaker abolitionist John Woolman (*The Journal of John Woolman*).

2 Tarter, "Go North!" 83–98.

3 Cathy Walling in Emily et al., *Reflections by Five Quaker Elders*.

4 Boulding, *One Small Plot of Heaven*, 172.

5 Steere, *On Listening to Another*, 14. This is the printed text of Douglas Steere's 1955 Swarthmore Lecture addressed to Britain Yearly Meeting. It was published in England under the title of *Where Words Come From* (1955).

6 North Carolina Yearly Meeting (Conservative) of the Religious Society of Friends, *Faith and Practice*, 26.

Chapter 4: The Spiritual Formation of the Elder

1 Bownas, *A Description of the Qualifications Necessary*, 4.

2 Ulanov, *Cinderella and Her Sisters*, 81.

3 Loring, *Listening Spirituality Vol. II*, 143–44.

4 Bownas, *A Description of the Qualifications Necessary*, 3.

5 Penington, "Some Directions to the Panting Soul," 486.

6 Tom Fox was a Quaker from Baltimore Yearly Meeting and a member of the Christian Peacemaker Teams in Iraq. For more about the legacy of Tom Fox's life among Friends, see Susan Corson-Finnerty, "Reflections on the Witness of Tom Fox," *Friends Journal* (May 1, 2006), https://www.friendsjournal.org/2006044/; Peggy O'Neill, "Being a Friendly Adult Presence in the Lives of Young Friends: What Would Tom Fox Do?" *Friends Journal* (July 1, 2007), https://www.friendsjournal.org/2007082/.

7 Walling and Emily, *Spiritual Accompaniment*, 24.

8 Taber, "Contemporary Examples of Eldering," 19.

9 Wilson, *Essays on the Quaker Vision of Gospel Order*, 106.

10 Brown, "The Right Way to Disagree."

11 Angela York Crane and Elaine Emily, shared with permission for use in this book.

12 Fell, "An Epistle to Convinced but not yet Crucified Friends, in 1656," 110.

13 Rustin, "In Apprehension How Like a God!"

14 We are grateful to Angela York Crane for her contribution to this section.

15 Nouwen, "Yearning for Perfect Love."

16 Recollection of Elaine Emily from an unknown source.

Chapter 5: Care of the Meeting as a Body Gathered by God: The Work of an Elder

1 Cronk, *Gospel Order*, 5–6.

2 Cronk, *Gospel Order*, 7–8.

3 Gates, *Members One of Another*.

4 Harper, "Nurturing the Spiritual Life of the Meeting," 25, 33.

5 Barnett, "Spiritual Eldership."

6 Keefe-Perry, "Tentmaker, Tailor."

7 Wilson, *Memoir*, 227.

8 Ferris, *Resistance and Obedience to God*, 51–52. We are grateful to Lu and Kenn Harper for reminding us of David Ferris's journal.

9 Gordon Bishop in Emily et al., *Reflections by Five Quaker Elders*.

10 Sánchez-Eppler, "Bible Half Hour."

11 Routledge, *Living Eldership*, pp. 20, 24.

12 Jan de Voogd, as cited in Australia Yearly Meeting, *This We Can Say*, 85.

13 Routledge, *Living Eldership*, 13.

14 Karen Reixach, "Recording as a Form of Eldering," 7.

15 Taber, *The Prophetic Stream*, 27. Taber's reference to Robert Barclay is from Dean Freiday, ed., *Barclay's Apology in Modern English* (Philadelphia, 1967), 253.

16 Francis D. Hole, letter to Ellie Schacter, in Hole and Shacter, *A Little Journal of Devotions*, 4.

17 Mary Rose O'Reilley, "Deep Listening," 18.

18 Emily, "The Quaker Practice of Traveling with an Elder."

19 Samuel Bownas, as cited in Taber, "Introduction," xxviii.

20 Job Scott, "Journal of the Life, Travels, &c of Job Scott," in *The Works of that Eminent Minister of the Gospel, Job Scott* (Philadelphia, J. Comly, 1831) vol. 1, 178–80, as cited in Harper, "Nurturing the Spiritual Life of the Meeting," 28.

[21] Susan Smith, "Overview," in Ohio Yearly Meeting, *So That You Come Behind in No Gift*, 2.

[22] Routledge, *Living Eldership*, 46.

[23] Larrabee, *Spirit-Led Eldering*, 22–23.

[24] Fitz-Hugh, "Friends and Conflict."

[25] Sanchez-Eppler, "Bible Half Hour."

[26] Lape, "A Case for Eldering and Discipline," 10–11.

[27] Samuel Bownas, as cited in Taber, "Introduction," xxvii–xxix.

[28] O'Reilley, *Radical Presence: Teaching as Contemplative Practice*, 29.

[29] Bruce Neumann, personal communication with the authors.

[30] Walling and Emily, *Spiritual Accompaniment*, 19.

[31] Carol Holmes Alpern and Ann Davidson, description of Comforters, Radiators, and Stopping By, a Ministry of Presence workshop held at Powell House September 15–17, 2006.

[32] Kelly, "Holding Space," *Spark*, 4–5.

[33] Ramos, "The Gift of Traveling with Each Other," 5.

Chapter 6: The Elder's Work: Frameworks for Practice and Understanding

[1] The framework of "before, during, and after meeting for worship" that we flesh out in this section was inspired by a handout developed by Katharine and Ken Jacobsen for a retreat they led for Elders from New York and New England Yearly Meetings in December 2012. Katharine and Ken based their handout on the form of eldership practiced in Ohio Yearly Meeting (Conservative). For more about the retreat, see Appendix 6: Building up the Life of Our Meetings.

[2] Cadbury, "Thoughts on Eldering" 6.

[3] Augustine, *Confessions* 1.1.5.

[4] Cadbury, "My Personal Religion."

[5] Routh, *Memoir*, 215.

Interlude 7: Eldering as a Decolonizing Action

[1] Woolman, *The Journal of John Woolman*.

Chapter 7: Traveling in the Ministry with an Elder

[1] Wilson, *Memoir*, 207.

[2] Harper, "Nurturing the Spiritual Life of the Meeting," 25.

[3] Carolyn Schodt, as cited in Philadelphia Yearly Meeting Spiritual Formation Collaborative, "Elders and Eldering."

[4] Walling and Emily, *Spiritual Accompaniment*, 12–13.

Interlude 10: Accompanying Traveling Minister Christopher Sammond as an Elder

[1] Fell, "An Epistle to Convinced but not yet Crucified Friends, in 1656," 110.

Chapter 8: Envisioning a Quaker Culture of Eldering

[1] Pomeroy, "Letting Go of the Term 'Elder,'" 4.

[2] Routledge, *Living Eldership*, 28.

[3] Smith, "Overview," 2.

[4] Larrabee, *Spirit-Led Eldering*, 11.

[5] Jenny Routledge, *Living Eldership*, 31–32.

[6] We are grateful to Christopher Sammond for the information he provided for this section.

[7] For more information, see New York Yearly Meeting, "Meetings for Discernment," https://www.nyym.org/content/meetings-discernment.

[8] Pacific Yearly Meeting, "Epistle."

Appendix 1: The Process of Writing This Book

[1] Walling and Emily, *Spiritual Accompaniment*.

Appendix 5: Eldering via Zoom

[1] See Jan Hoffman's 1988 quote on "Quaker Decision-Making" in New England Yearly Meeting, *Interim Faith and Practice*, sec. 3.09, https://neym.org/faith-and-practice/decision-making:

> The sense of the meeting is not unanimity—everyone present need not agree with the action being taken. I have had the experience of concurring in a sense of meeting with which I disagreed, knowing it was the sense of the meeting. I have wept, wishing the meeting could go further than it was ready to go, but clearly it was not ready to do so.
>
> When I am disappointed with a sense of the meeting, I try not to give much attention to why we didn't do more, but to focus on openness to the next step, based on the experience that will follow carrying out the clarity we did reach. I also try and listen to the love within me that accepts people in my faith community for what they are, and pray that God will use and transform us all. Let me also say how much I appreciate the further light we get from each other along the way from monthly meetings to quarterly meetings to Yearly Meeting—we learn and are challenged by concerns beyond our local community of faith.
>
> As I see it, there is only one necessary query: Is the Spirit present? Is new experience teaching me that it is present in places I have previously thought it couldn't be? If so, maybe I need to change.

Appendix 6: Building Up the Life of Our Meetings

[1] This quote is based on a passage by Earl C. Kelley in his 1951 book *The Workshop Way of Learning*.

Appendix 9: The Challenges of Accompanying Ministers in Their Humanity

[1] I word it this way because I understand my work as an elder is to accompany ministry rather than a given minister. By the nature of the work, when I accompany ministry, that also includes walking with the minister.

Also available from Inner Light Books

Memoir of the Life and Religious Labors
of Lloyd Lee Wilson
By Lloyd Lee Wilson
       ISBN 978-1-7370112-3-1(hardcover)
       ISBN 978-1-7370112-4-8, (paperback)
       ISBN 978-1-7370112-5-5, (eBook)

Messages to Meetings
by Brian Drayton
       ISBN 978-1-7370112-0-0 (hardcover)
       ISBN 978-1-7370112-1-7 (paperback)
       ISBN 978-1-7370112-2-4 (eBook)

Movings of Divine Love: The Love of God in the
Letters of John Woolman
by Drew Lawson
       ISBN 978-1-7346300-3-9 (hardcover)
       ISBN 978-1-7346300-4-6 (paperback)
       ISBN 978-1-7346300-5-3 (eBook)

A Call to Friends: Faithful Living in Desperate Times
by Marty Grundy
       ISBN 978–1-7346300–6-0 (hardcover)
       ISBN 978–1-7346300–7-7 (paperback)
       ISBN 978–1-7346300–8-4 (eBook)

Surrendering into Silence: Quaker Prayer Cycles
by David Johnson
       ISBN 978–1-7346300–0-8 (hardcover)
       ISBN 978–1-7346300–1-5 (paperback)
       ISBN 978–1-7346300–2-2 (eBook)

A Guide to Faithfulness Groups
by Marcelle Martin
       ISBN 978-1-7328239-4-5 (hardcover)
       ISBN 978-1-7328239-5-2 (paperback)
       ISBN 978-1-7328239-6-9 (eBook)

A Word from the Lost: Remarks on James Nayler's Love to the Lost
by David Lewis
       ISBN 978-1-7328239-7-6 (hardcover)
       ISBN 978-1-7328239-8-3 (paperback)
       ISBN 978-1-7328239-9-0 (eBook)

William Penn's 'Holy Experiment'
by James Proud
       ISBN 978-0-9998332-9-2 (hardcover)
       ISBN 978-1-7328239-3-8 (paperback)

In the Stillness: Poems, prayers, reflections
by Elizabeth Mills

> ISBN 978-1-7328239-0-7 (hardcover)
> ISBN 978-1-7328239-1-4 (paperback)
> ISBN 978-1-7328239-2-1 (eBook)

Walk Humbly, Serve Boldly: Modern Quakers as Everyday Prophets
by Margery Post Abbott

> ISBN 978-0-9998332-6-1 (hardcover)
> ISBN 978-0-9998332-7-8 (paperback)
> ISBN 978-0-9998332-8-5 (eBook)

Primitive Quakerism Revived
by Paul Buckley

> ISBN 978-0-9998332-2-3 (hardcover)
> ISBN 978-0-9998332-3-0 (paperback)
> ISBN 978-0-9998332-5-4 (eBook)

Primitive Christianity Revived
by William Penn
Translated into Modern English by Paul Buckley

> ISBN 978-0-9998332-0-9 (hardcover)
> ISBN 978-0-9998332-1-6 (paperback)
> ISBN 978-0-9998332-4-7 (eBook)

Jesus, Christ and Servant of God
Meditations on the Gospel According to John
by David Johnson

> ISBN 978–0–9970604–6–1 (hardcover)
> ISBN 978–0–9970604–7–8 (paperback)
> ISBN 978–0–9970604–8–5 (eBook)

The Anti-War
by Douglas Gwyn

> ISBN 978-0-9970604-3-0 (hardcover)
> ISBN 978-0-9970604-4-7 (paperback)
> ISBN 978-0-9970604-5-4 (eBook)

Our Life Is Love, the Quaker Spiritual Journey
by Marcelle Martin

> ISBN 978-0-9970604-0-9 (hardcover)
> ISBN 978-0-9970604-1-6 (paperback)
> ISBN 978-0-9970604-2-3 (eBook)

A Quaker Prayer Life
by David Johnson

> ISBN 978-0-9834980-5-6 (hardcover)
> ISBN 978-0-9834980-6-3 (paperback)
> ISBN 978-0-9834980-7-0 (eBook)

The Essential Elias Hicks
by Paul Buckley

> ISBN 978-0-9834980-8-7 (hardcover)
> ISBN 978-0-9834980-9-4 (paperback)
> ISBN 978-0-9970604-9-2 (eBook)

The Journal of Elias Hicks
edited by Paul Buckley

> ISBN 978-0-9797110-4-6 (hardcover)
> ISBN 978-0-9797110-5-3 (paperback)

Dear Friend: The Letters and Essays of Elias Hicks
edited by Paul Buckley

> ISBN 978-0-9834980-0-1 (hardcover)
> ISBN 978-0-9834980-1-8 (paperback)

The Early Quakers and 'the Kingdom of God'
by Gerard Guiton

> ISBN 978-0-9834980-2-5 (hardcover)
> ISBN 978-0-9834980-3-2 (paperback)
> ISBN 978-0-9834980-4-9 (eBook)

John Woolman and the Affairs of Truth
edited by James Proud

> ISBN 978-0-9797110-6-0 (hardcover)
> ISBN 978-0-9797110-7-7 (paperback)

Cousin Ann's Stories for Children by Ann Preston
edited by Richard Beards
illustrated by Stevie French

> ISBN 978-0-9797110-8-4 (hardcover),
> ISBN 978-0-9797110-9-1 (paperback)

Counsel to the Christian-Traveller: also Meditations and Experiences
by William Shewen

> ISBN 978-0-9797110-0-8 (hardcover)
> ISBN 978-0-9797110-1-5 (paperback)

www.ingramcontent.com/pod-product-compliance
Lightning Source LLC
Chambersburg PA
CBHW030910060726
47591CB00005B/1484